Kinetic Kaleidoscope

Exploring Movement and Energy in the Visual Arts

Gail Neary Herman, Ph.D.
Patricia Hollingsworth, Ed.D.

Zephyr Press
Tucson, Arizona

Kinetic Kaleidoscope
Exploring Movement and Energy in the Visual Arts

Grades 3-8

© 1992 Zephyr Press

ISBN: 0-913705-68-3

Editor: Susan Newcomer
Book Design and Production: Nancy Taylor
Cover Design: Michelle Gallardo

Cover: *Oil Pastel* by Neal Parks, 1987
        Artist's collection

Zephyr Press
P.O. Box 13448
Tucson, AZ 85732-3448

Contents

Art Reproductions v
Introduction 1
Kinesthetic Responses 5
I   Kinetic Energy Concepts 13
     Definitions of Energy 13
     The Kinesphere 14
        Activity 1: The Space Bubble 15
        Activity 2: The Box 16
        Activity 3: Space Ships 17
        Activity 4: Journal 18
     Planes and Directions in Space 19
        Activity 1: Four Directions 21
        Activity 2: Journal 22
     Review Activity 1: Shapes, Levels, Directions, Planes 22
     Review Activity 2: Journal 23
II Laban's Four Motion Factors 31
     Time 32
        Activity 1: Talking Time Drum 33
        Activity 2: Looking at Art 34
        Activity 3: Journal 34
     Space 35
        Activity 1: Exploring the Space Continuum 35
        Activity 2: Journal 37
        Activity 3: Looking at Space in Art 37
        Activity 4: Journal 38
     Force 39
        Activity 1: Sensing Weight 39
        Activity 2: Looking at Art 41
        Activity 3: Journal 41
     Flow 42
        Activity 1: Let's Flow 43
        Activity 2: Moving in Moon Space 44
        Activity 3: Looking at Art 45
        Activity 4: Journal 45
     Review Activity 1: Energy Words 46
     Review Activity 2: Journal 47
III Eight Effort Actions 51
     Float Activity 1: Hello...52
     Float Activity 2: Looking at Art..52
     Glide Activity 1: Hello..53
     Glide Activity 2: Looking at Art..53
     Dab Activity 1: Hello..54
     Dab Activity 2: Mime..54
     Dab Activity 3: Looking at Art..55

Flick Activity 1: Hello...55
Flick Activity 2: Looking at Art...56
Flick Activity 3: Moving with Art...56
Wring Activity 1: Hello...56
Wring Activity 2: Looking at Art...57
Press Activity 1: Hello..57
Press Activity 2: Looking at Art..58
Punch Activity 1: Hello...58
Punch Activity 2: Looking at Art...59
Slash Activity 1: Hello..59
Slash Activity 2: Looking at Art..60
Effort Action Review Activities..61
    Review Activitiy 1: Contrasting Artwork.................................61
    Review Activity 2: Robot..61
    Review Activity 3: Flick a Fly...62
    Review Activity 4: Looking at Art..63
    Review Activity 5: Interpreting Art with Music.........................63
    Review Activity 6: Journal..64
    Review Activity 7: Explosive Shapes and Melting Shapes........65
    Review Activity 8: Explosive Shapes with a Partner.................66
    Review Activity 9: Wring and Press......................................67
IV Kinetic Energy in the Arts Activities...71
    Activity 1: A Moveable Feast—Motion Factors.......................71
    Activity 2: Interpreting Art—Effort Actions...........................72
    Activity 3: Journal—Motion and Effort Actions......................73
    Activity 4: Conductor—Efforts and Sounds...........................74
    Activity 5: Journal—Dab and Flick.....................................75
    Activity 6: Gong—Press, Wring, Glide, Float........................75
    Activity 7: Journal—Sustained Energy.................................76
    Activity 8: Kinetic Sculpture—Sustained and Quick Energy.......76
    Activity 9: Sound Screen—Movement and Sound....................77
    Activity 10: Looking at Art—The Sound of Art.......................79
    Activity 11: Journal—Sound Screen....................................80
    Activity 12: Interpreting Drawings—Voice Movement..............80
    Activity 13: Journal—Energy Cards....................................83
    Activity 14: Chicka-Boom—Vocal Interpretation....................83
    Activity 15: Journal—Intrepretation, Memory and Mood..........85
    Activity 16: Be the Thing—Interpretation and Transformation....86
    Activity 17: Journal—Writing Dialogue................................87
    Activity 18: Journal—Transforming Text...............................87
Conclusion..91
Glossary...92
References...95

Art Reproductions

Alphabetical Listing of Artwork by Artist with Key Movement Qualities

Alexander, Francis • *Ralph Wheelock's Farm* (glide, hortizontal) 10
Brown, W. H. • *Bareback Riders* (angular shapes, dabs) 23
Cézanne, Paul • *Still Life* (straight lines) 70
Chambers, Thomas • *Felucca off Gibraltar* (slash, flick) 68
Constable, John • *A View of Salisbury Cathedral* (glide, float, vertical) 48
Dufy, Raoul • *Basin at Deauville* (vertical, flick) 11
Eakins, Thomas • *The Biglin Brothers Racing* (glide) vi
Fantin-Latour, Henri • *Still Life* (controlled, bound) 69
Feininger, Lyonel • *Zirchow VII* (direct, straight lines) 28
Gauguin, Paul • *Self-Portrait* (curves, slashes) 27
Hartley, Marsden • *The Aero* (punch, slash, wavy) 50
Heade, Martin • *Cattleya Orchid and Three Brazilian Hummingbirds* (bound, float) 48
Herman, Leta • *Water* (free, unbound) 29
Hockney, David • *Sun* (diagonal, bound, glide, direct) 10
Homer, Winslow • *Right and Left* (flick, slash, free, urgent) 26
Kandinsky, Wassily • *Improvisation 31 (Sea Battle)* (curvy, slash) 30
Klimt, Gustav • *Baby (Cradle)* (busy, curving, indirect) 27
Kollwitz, Käthe • *Self-Portrait with a Pencil* (quick) 25
Kuhn, Walt • *The White Clown* (soft, continuous curves) 24
Louis, Morris • *133* (press, control, sustained) 10
Magritte, René • *The Blank Signature* (vertical, flick, dab) 30
Manet, Edouard • *The Races* (diagonal, quick) 11
Matisse, Henri • *Beasts of the Sea* (curved, indirect) 24
Matisse, Henri • *Still Life with Sleeping Woman* (slash, dab, curved) 49
Mondrian, Piet • *Diamond Painting in Red, Yellow, Blue* (vertical, hortizontal) 12
Monet, Claude • *Woman with a Parasol–Madame Monet and Her Son* (flick, dab) 28
Motherwell, Robert • *Reconciliation Elegy* (slash) 29
Neary, Tom • *By a Nose* (saggital) 12
Nolde, Emil • *The Prophet* (strong, reserved, vertical) vi
Parks, Neal • *Oil Pastel* (light, controlled, bound) .... cover
Peto, John Frederick • *The Old Violin* (diagonal, bound) vi
Picasso, Pablo • *Still Life* (dab, flick, direct, curved) 24
Pollock, Jackson • *Number 1, 1950 (Lavender Mist)* (flick, dab) 25
Rosebrooks, Ann • *Kitchen III* (diagonal, dabs, curves) 70
Rousseau, Henri • *The Equatorial Jungle* (flick, slash) 69
Rubens, Peter Paul • *A Lion* (flick, strong, sustained) 26
Ryder, Albert Pinkham • *Siegfried and the Rhine Maidens* (wring) 50
Seurat, Georges • *The Lighthouse at Honfleur* (dabs, diagonal) 49
Twachtman, John Henry • *Winter Harmony* (soft, indirect, float, free) 27
Utrillo, Maurice • *The Church at Saint-Severin* (vertical, saggital) 11
Vuillard, Edouard • *Woman in a Striped Dress* (flick, dab) 50
Weyden, Rogier van der • *Portrait of a Lady* (bound, controlled) 28
Weyden, Rogier van der • *St. George and the Dragon* (diagonal) 12

The Old Violin, c. 1890
John Frederick Peto
National Gallery of Art, Washington, D.C.

The Prophet, 1912
Emil Nolde
National Gallery of Art, Washington, D.C.

The Biglin Brothers Racing, 1873
Thomas Eakins
National Gallery of Art, Washington, D.C.

Introduction

Every art form appeals to a special sense, a unique instrument of artistic appreciation—music to the ear, visual art to the eye, dance to the kinesthetic sense—or so it seems. Hoping to instill in children an appreciation of the visual arts, adults often direct them to *look*. Yet children have irrepressible energy. Asked to listen to music, they automatically move to its rhythms unless some unsympathetic adult forces them to sit still, "the better to appreciate it." But the child's natural movement opens another kind of sense interaction with the music, strengthening the child's relationship to the work and deepening the child's appreciation.

The visual arts may seem to appeal to fewer senses than music. After all, the visual arts—at least most of them—are static. When we look at them they make no noise or movement, and the ubiquitous museum signs forbid their being touched. The sole source for cultivating appreciation of the visual arts seems to be sight itself and perhaps participation in creating artworks. Many books have been written to help teachers foster appreciation through these means.

Kinetic Kaleidoscope has the same general purpose, but its strategy is different. Our main thesis is that works of art contain within their frozen frames an inner dynamism and energy that an individual's perceptual apparatus can translate into kinesthetic impressions, movement, and sound. Through this translation a child's natural energies can interact with the artwork through multiple sensory experiences, enriching and deepening art appreciation.

Definitions

According to the *Random House Dictionary of the English Language*, the word *kinesthetic* comes from two Greek words: *kinein*, meaning "to move or set in motion," and *aisthesis*, meaning "sensation or feeling." Kinesthetic means literally sensing or feeling the motion. The sensation of movement or strain in muscles, tendons, or joints can be thought to include feelings deep within the organ muscles of our body. *Webster's Third New International Dictionary of the English Language* includes in the definition of *kinesthetic* a notion of "motor memory." We say we can have memories of kinesthetic events that we can manipulate much as we do words and images.

 Kinetic Kaleidoscope provides the reader with strategies for helping students experience their own multisensory responsiveness to the visual

arts. Readers learn how to arouse in children a totally different way of interacting with art. Involving the whole body, the kinesthetic "muscular" response engages students not only at the intellectual level of classroom presentation and discussion but also at the physical and emotional levels. Kinesthetic response opens and extends the pathways for enriched conceptual understanding and aesthetic appreciation.

Reasons to Encourage Kinesthetic Learning

Kinesthetic learning has four main benefits: it strengthens memory, it enriches conceptualization and deepens understanding, it promotes creativity, and it expands the potential for aesthetic communication. Physical learning—such as typing, tying a shoelace, and playing the piano—is not forgotten as quickly as many isolated facts. Many acquired physical skills are, as people say, "just like riding a bicycle." Twenty years after one's last carefree, self-assured bike ride, an adult mounts the once-obedient machine, fearful that the old knowledge of self-propulsion is as fleeting as youth. Cautiously, without rehearsal, the cyclist pushes off. The muscles and tendons take over. Neurons fire along the old neural pathways still etched in the nervous system. The cyclist is under way, unsteadily at first, but then with the gleeful, exuberant feeling of youth. The body has not forgotten.

The body's memory can be used to assist aesthetic memory (as well as memory in general). The student told to look at a Seurat will see the points of paint out of which the scene is composed. But the learning is often as brief as the lesson. Mere sight often proves insufficient to fix concepts in mind. However, the student who performs dabbing movements to represent pointillism, thereby associating the meaning of the concept with kinesthetic impressions, will increase the neural pathways for recollection and be more apt to recall the meaning in the future.

Organization

Kinetic Kaleidoscope is designed primarily for teachers, but parents and other adults who hope to stimulate children's enthusiasm for the visual arts will find it a valuable resource. After a brief examination of the theoretical background, the text has four main parts: the first three are designed to give students a movement vocabulary and a repertoire of movements with which to respond to artworks. The last section presents field-tested exercises designed to expand students' responsiveness to art. Because *Kinetic Kaleidoscope* is written for practitioners, each section presents activities to encourage kinesthetic and visual interaction.

Artwork and Materials

Readers will find visuals, exercises, and detailed instructions to assist them in preparing each activity. Sections titled "Let's Move!" or "Let's Look!"—printed in italics—provide suggested directions and explanations for teachers to use when speaking directly to students. You do not need to quote passages verbatim. They are meant to provide guidance only. We also encourage teachers to reproduce the textual materials freely for their students. They are for your use in the classroom.

Students will also need to look at works of art! Each activity has an artwork reproduced in the text to illustrate main concepts. Readers will also be able to find many other examples for themselves. Students respond better to large color reproductions typically available from a local museum, library, or district resource center. You may also find good color reproductions in art books or as posters, slides, or postcards available from museum gift shops and mail-order catalogs. The National Gallery in Washington, D.C., has the least expensive good color prints we could find. To purchase inexpensive prints of artwork from the National Gallery, write for a catalog at this address: National Gallery of Art, Mail Order Department, 2000 B South Club Dr., Landover, MD 27085. When choosing works to study, be sure to select ones that have good color and high-quality printing.

Exposure to art helps students become comfortable with looking at art. The more exposure the better. When focusing on a single work, use an easel positioned in the front of the room so all can see. You might also consider a bulletin board for displaying art postcards and other art-related items.

An Invitation to Joyful Reading

We encourage readers to try the exercises themselves. In this way you will find your own responsiveness to the inner energy in artworks, enhance your own enjoyment, and become a more creative, skillful, and committed guide in the artistic development of children.

Kinesthetic Responses

In a speech at the University of Connecticut in 1980, Elliot Eisner—a leading proponent of aesthetic education—suggested that sensation, the "stuff" of the senses, is the raw material of imagination. A commonly held view—a view we authors share—is that creativity and imagination are associated in an important way. Further, we believe that the arts, which are repositories of human imaginative production, are in some fashion endowed with a special potency for stimulating, cultivating, and developing imaginative and creative thought. We suspect that much creative thinking derives from nondiscursive elements—feelings and sensations—that fill out and enrich the content of experience. Yet many programs for fostering creative thinking and even art appreciation tend to rely heavily on the discursive mode, neglecting nonverbal experience. To some extent, these programs are self-defeating.

Kinesthetic Responses in Thinking

In *Conceptual Blockbusting: A Guide to Better Ideas*, James L. Adams writes: "If one thinks purely verbally . . . there will be little imagery available for the solving of problems concerning shapes and forms. If visual imagery is present, the imagination will be much more useful, but still not as potent as if the other senses are also present" (60).

Of the senses typically unrepresented in programs for fostering creative thinking, the kinesthetic sense is the most neglected. "Kinesthetic sense" refers to the feelings we receive from our muscles, joints, tendons, organs, and skin. Our kinesthetic sense helps us know texture, feelings, and spatial information. For example, the kinesthetic sense helps us know or recall our position in space, pathways we have taken, and feelings we have experienced.

Kinesthetic information may also play an important role in cognition. Albert Einstein's theories are recognized as models of higher-order cognitive thought. Discussing his own thinking processes in a letter to a friend, Einstein suggested in a surprisingly forceful passage that sense awareness—including muscular elements—was essential to his process of inquiry and theory construction.

> "The words or the language, as they are written or spoken, do not seem to play *any role* in my mechanism of thought. The psychical entities which seem to serve as elements in thought are certain signs and more or less clear images which can be 'voluntarily' reproduced and combined. . . . Taken from a psychological viewpoint, this combinatory play seems to be the essential feature in productive thought—before there is any connection with logical construction in words or other kinds of signs which can be communicated to others.
>
> "The above mentioned elements are, in my case, of visual and some of *muscular* type. Conventional words or other signs have to be sought for laboriously only in a secondary stage, when the mentioned associative play is sufficiently established and can be reproduced at will." (Quoted in Ghiselin, 45, emphasis ours)

We can cast Einstein's thoughts in more familiar terms. He was trying to "visualize" or "feel" his innovative ideas. Words came later, with much hard work. One might understand why. Creative thinkers at the frontier of human inquiry are pioneers forced to grope along previously untraveled and unmarked paths. When creative thinkers find themselves in completely unfamiliar territory in which their old concepts and theories no longer work as reliable guides, they sometimes draw upon other resources—images and visceral and muscular sensations—which are the raw material of creative ideas, hunches, intuitions, and inclinations. Nonverbal experience, as Einstein seems to be suggesting, is an insufficiently understood and, all too often, dismissed notion that is nevertheless a powerful informant of creative thought.

Kinesthetic or muscular elements of thought are familiar. For example, when we are on a waiting train and the train next to ours begins to move, we experience a feeling of motion. Although our train is not really moving, the movement sensations we experience are real. Some people also experience kinesthetic or muscular responses when given directions. They actually move their hands to the right or left or feel tugs and pulls in the direction they need to remember. Later, these muscular elements of thought may be recalled to help guide the traveler. This may be what people mean when they say they are "feeling their way" toward their destination.

Kinesthetic elements of thought also aid recollection of emotion. For example, an adult who has experienced a trauma in childhood may have no conscious recollection of the painful event. But years later, under safer circumstances, muscular responses akin to the ones felt during the trauma may be restimulated. Then memories of the traumatic event may come flooding back into consciousness.

Kinesthetic Responses in Acting

The famous director and acting coach Constantin Stanislavski referred to similar phenomena called "sensation memories," meaning that we remember what we have sensed visually, kinesthetically, and aurally (158–60). Stanislavski held that sense memories about movements and emotions are elements of experience that can be noted, stored, recalled, and manipulated just as words and visual elements are.

Kinesthetic Responses in Viewing Visual Art

In *The Aesthetic Attitude*, Herbert S. Langfeld summarized theories of German aestheticians of the late nineteenth and early twentieth centuries pertaining to people's "motor attitudes," "motor responses," "inner mimicry," "empathic response," and "tendencies toward movement" while looking at works of art (109–42). According to Langfeld, if we become aware of and then analyze our kinesthetic responses to art, we can "add to the depth and richness of our immediate experience, sharpen the critical function, and heighten the power of discrimination" in viewing art (120).

Langfeld credited his professor Karl Groos for first using the term "inner mimicry" to refer to actual sensations of emotion and movement (117). Langfeld also believed that many sensations accompanying art experience go unnoticed during the act of "aesthetic contemplation" but can be revealed or discovered later if one reflects on and analyzes the experience. To illustrate his point, Langfeld quoted C. Anstruther-Thomson, co-author with Vernon Lee of *Beauty and Ugliness*. Describing and analyzing her own movement response while viewing the *Venus de Milo*, Anstruther-Thomson realized that her body and muscles had reacted as if by reflex to mimic the balance and lift of the posture and stance of the statue.

Aestheticians refer to this tendency toward movement and motor response as an "empathic response." In German the term "Einfuhlung" means "feeling into" and is translated into English as "empathy." German aesthetician Theodore Lipps developed a theory of aesthetic perception based on the human ability to empathize or project ourselves into artworks. For example, upon viewing columns of the Parthenon, the perceiver may experience inner pressures akin to the pressures that one might imagine are being exerted downward on the columns from the roof and upward from the foundation as it resists the downward pressures.

The empathic response is familiar to all of us. Sometimes as we view a suspense thriller, we become absorbed in the lives of the characters, feeling a shortness of breath, heart palpitations, and a tendency to move as if we were the characters themselves. Perhaps, when we entered the theater, we were troubled by a mild backache. But as the cinematic events unfold, we get "caught up," and our awareness of our pain recedes from consciousness. Later, when the film has ended and we "come back to ourselves," the irritating pain resumes. Describing the film to a friend, we might exclaim, "My heart was pounding. I was so scared I nearly jumped out of my skin. I even forgot I had a backache."

Inner Mimicry Becomes Overt Movement

Asking students to become aware of the kinesthetic sensations and motor attitudes they experience while observing art will increase their insight and enjoyment, too. The activities in *Kinetic Kaleidoscope* have been field-tested in many schools. After working through the activities presented here, a fifth-grade class visited a large city museum. The curator was impressed by the students' involvement in the paintings and their obvious enjoyment. She recounted seeing two students standing in front of a Franz Kline painting, discussing the power of the horizontal and diagonal lines in terms of "firmness," "strength," "slashing," and "thrust"—the movement vocabulary of Rudolf Laban, introduced

in *Kinetic Kaleidoscope* to the reader. But what most amazed the curator was not the students' prolific vocabulary but the way they stood—or rather moved—before the painting. They used their arms to express the painting's powerful movement. Another student, talking about an Impressionist's work, moved his fingers in quick dabbing motions as if he could actually feel the strokes the artist was painting.

There is a "muscular element" to experiencing and remembering as well as to making art. We inhabit our whole body, and our whole body is a source and reservoir of experience. What better way to respond to our world than with our whole body? Teaching children to value their kinesthetic reactions can be as great a source of satisfaction for the teacher and concerned adult as it is for the child. As children learn to translate the elements of a work of art—line, shape, texture, color—into movement, they can come to "know" the work in ways that deepen and enrich their aesthetic experience.

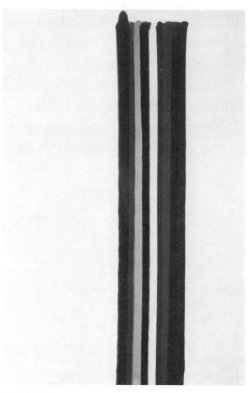

Sun, 1973
David Hockney
National Gallery of Art, Washington, D.C.

133, 1962
Morris Louis
National Gallery of Art, Washington, D.C.

Ralph Wheelock's Farm, 1822
Francis Alexander
National Gallery of Art, Washington, D.C.

The Church at Saint-Severin, c. 1913
Maurice Utrillo
National Gallery of Art, Washington, D.C.

The Races, 1865
Edouard Manet
National Gallery of Art, Washington, D.C.

Basin at Deauville, 1937
Raoul Dufy
National Gallery of Art, Washington, D.C.

Diamond Painting in Red, Yellow, Blue, 1921-25
Piet Mondrian
National Gallery of Art, Washington, D.C.

St. George and the Dragon, 1432
Rogier van der Weyden
National Gallery of Art, Washington, D.C.

By a Nose, 1945
Tom Neary
Private collection

I Kinetic Energy Concepts

To describe the inner energy and motion in artworks, we first need a vocabulary. This vocabulary will be derived from several sources: from ordinary language, from science and other disciplines, and from the arts themselves, especially the movement arts. We begin with *energy*, a term fundamental to our discussion.

Definitions of Energy

Energy is a familiar term. We speak of electrical energy, of the energy stored in a good breakfast cereal, of the energy of the sun. The term also has technical meanings. "Energy" can refer to what physicists call "potential energy," the capacity to do work. "Energy" can also refer to actual work manifested in motion or what physicists call "kinetic energy."

In addition to the energy found in the natural world, human beings feel energy within themselves. Sometimes they feel sluggish and dispirited and say they have low energy. At other times they feel vigorous and vital and say they have high energy. Dancer and aesthetician Rudolf Laban referred to this energy in people as "effort, which springs from our inner impulses, desires, intentions, moods, and drives, and which manifests itself in the movements of our body" (*Modern Educational Dance*, 114). For Laban, bodily energy and movement are linked. When talking about human energy, we will use his terms. In *Kinetic Kaleidoscope*, however, we also want to talk about the energy in artworks. Since paintings are typically motionless, they would seem by definition to be devoid of energy. Yet viewers often react to works of art as if their surfaces were not frozen in time.

In ***The Biglin Brothers Racing*** by Thomas Eakins (p. vi), for example, the viewer sees two brothers, arms extended, just before they reverse stroke and pull the oars back toward their chests. Somehow the brothers' posture and the anticipation of their exertion lead viewers to transcend the frozen frame of the painting and see a scene unfolding before their eyes, in many respects much as some might witness such a scene taking place on a real river. Although the scene is presented on a static surface, viewers can sense the energy in the painting.

In *Kinetic Kaleidoscope*, the capacity of a work of art to produce physiological and emotional responses is what we call kinetic energy. Brush strokes leave the imprint of the painter's thought and movement. In a sense, the artwork is a storehouse of the artist's energy, waiting to be revitalized within ourselves. Emil Nolde's **The Prophet** (p. vi) is a good example of a work that can evoke physiological and emotional reactions. The work is often described by students as "weighty," "sad," yet "strong." The dark mass at the bottom right and the direction of the lines seem to pull the viewer down. The eyes reveal a pensive sadness, but there is an overall sense of strength in the prophet's face, according to many students. No matter how it is interpreted, Nolde's **Prophet** evokes strong expressive energy. This kind of energy begins with the artist and generates energy in the viewer.

The Kinesphere

Since *Kinetic Kaleidoscope* recommends movement exercises, each student needs a defined safe space. All people have a kinesphere, a "self space" surrounding them. The kinesphere is like an imaginary encompassing ball or bubble that can provide the space for safe personal movement. It expands or shrinks as needed.

The following activities introduce children to their kinespheres. Their exploration of levels, directions, and shapes in space begins within the kinesphere and will help them feel "movement spaces." The children will use their movement knowledge and vocabulary later when they examine and discuss works of art. Eventually students will become familiar with a whole range of movement in their kinespheres and around the axis or center of their bodies. The following is a chart of some of the words they will encounter.

Shapes:	Round, twisted, thin, wide, pointy, curvy, angular
Levels:	High, medium, low
Directions:	Forward and back in the sagittal plane
	Sideways in the horizontal plane
	Up and down in the vertical plane
	Across in the diagonal plane

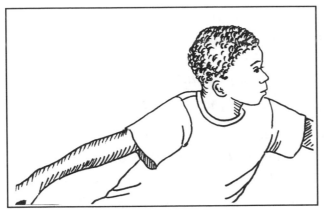

The kinesphere is also an emotionally safe place for a child to express ideas and feelings through movement. In the following activities, there are no wrong ways to respond so long as children move safely inside their bubbles. Their kinespheres should be their sanctuary of exploration. Each child should feel free to explore ideas, feelings, and movement, secure in the knowledge that each way of responding will be appreciated.

Kinesphere Activity 1: The Space Bubble

To the Teacher

The objective of the Space Bubble is to teach your students the concept of the kinesphere. You will need a drum for part of this activity. As you pronounce the word "kinesphere," emphasize each of its three syllables. Beat the drum and have the children clap at the same time, one beat for each syllable. Each asterisk below represents a beat of the drum.

Let's Move!

♦ *I want each of you to stand. Imagine you are in your own "space bubble." Find a space in the room where you can reach out with your arms and not touch anyone else. This bubble is your kinesphere, your own personal space for the activities we are going to do. Examine it carefully. If you notice any wrinkles in it, pretend to smooth them out.*

♦ *Now, I want you to clap out the syllables of the word kin-es-sphere. When I beat the drum *, clap as high as you can as we all say kin*-es*-sphere*. Now clap as low to the ground as you can. Kin*-es*-sphere*. Now, clap in the middle. Kin*-es*-sphere*. These are the levels of your kinesphere. We'll use these levels in many of the activities that follow.*

- *Now look down and find a spot on the floor that you can see. That's your "center spot." One foot should always be on your center spot while we are doing kinesphere activities. Now, let's examine the bubble carefully. If you notice any wrinkles, pretend to smooth them out again.*

- *Next, let's move with our feet. Stamp kin*-es*-sphere*.*

- *Imagine you have a paintbrush in each hand. Now, reach one arm out to the middle level in front of you. Paint some lines on the surface of your space bubble. Remember to keep at least one foot on your center spot on the floor. When I beat the drum, bend or lunge into the space low in front of you. Freeze that shape! Imagine for a second what a person might be doing in this position without a paintbrush. If you enter someone else's space, move away so you have enough space of your own without entering another person's space.*

- *Now, stand up. While standing and facing me, reach down behind you as far as you can. Paint some lines behind you. When I beat the drum, touch one side of your bubble. Now run your hand along that side as far back as you can. Freeze that shape! Imagine what activity a person might be doing in this position.*

- *Now paint rainbows overhead. Then paint a rainbow from low behind you to over your head to low in front of you. Can you paint a rainbow all around your waist?*

- *You have just learned about your kinesphere, and you have explored its three levels: high, middle, and low. You have used your space behind, in front, and on the sides of you.*

Kinesphere Activity 2: The Box

Let's Move!

♦ *Imagine that your bubble has turned into a box so that it has square corners. Stand with your feet wide apart inside your box. Reach across up high in front so that you can touch the top corner of your space box. Now, draw an imaginary diagonal line downward across the front of the box to the opposite low front corner near the floor.*

♦ *Use your other arm and reach diagonally across your body to the other low corner of your box. Now, draw a line diagonally upward across your body to the opposite high corner at the top of the box. Stretch your shape high.*

♦ *Now, stretch one arm up high in front and to the side of you box. If it is your right arm, stretch it to the right high front corner. Take your other arm and stretch it to the low back side behind you in the corner. That is an open diagonal stretch.* [Students can also explore making horizontal and vertical pathways with their arms and bodies within their boxes.]

♦ *Now that we have explored all the regions of your box—high, medium, low, front, back, sides, and diagonals—remember one place you stretched and then fantasize one unusual object you might have found there or one activity you might have been doing there.*

♦ *Now, let's share all the activities and places that came to mind as you moved in the various directions and levels.*

Kinesphere Activity 3: Space Shapes

To the Teacher

The objective of this activity is to encourage students to explore shapes inside their kinespheres. Instead of relying on vision to draw shapes, the students will use their bodies to assume shapes.

As they use their bodies, encourage them to notice their feelings and their visual imagery. Ask, "What pictures come to mind?" In this way associations are developed that frame an expanded and more holistic awareness of the space they occupy. You will need a drum or tone block to give directions.

Let's Move!

♦ *Today we will explore making shapes inside your kinesphere. Find a space where you are not touching anyone else. Now find your center spot and remember to keep one foot on it. Okay, reach to the farthest point of your kinesphere. When I beat the drum twice, make a shape, any shape, with your body. Then freeze. Ready! Go* *!*

◆ *Good. Now hold it steady. Even if you are on one foot, freeze it. Good. Some of you even have frozen eyes. That makes you look like a statue.*

◆ *Now, in your kinesphere, try to make the strangest shape you can. Wait until I beat the drum. Ready! Go* *!*

◆ *Great! I see some very interesting shapes. Relax. Now, make the most angular, pointy, sticking-out shape you can. Some of you might use the space behind you. Ready! Go* *! Now freeze! Good! I see everyone frozen in space. Picture your shape in your mind's eye. I see some really jagged shapes. I see several different levels—high, medium, low. I see shapes with angles—angular shapes. I also see straight shapes.*

◆ *Notice how you feel in these positions. What images come to mind? Okay, relax.*

◆ *Now, make another jagged, prickly shape on a different level. Try using parts of your body you haven't used before. Think about all your joints—your many finger joints and your neck, hips, and knees. Ready! Go* *!*

◆ *Think about what you could be doing in this shape. What do you feel like? What kind of object might you be? When I come and tap you, tell the class what you might be.* [Tap several students and ask each one what he or she might be. Repeat the answer so the whole class can hear.]

◆ *When I beat the drum again, make a very curved, twisted shape. Ready! Go* *!*

◆ *Now, in your kinesphere make a smooth, curvy shape on a different level. If you were low before, make a high or medium shape now. Remember to freeze your shape. Ready! Go* *!*

◆ *Notice how you feel in these positions. What might you be doing or who might you be? Okay, relax.*

Kinesphere Activity 4: Journal

To the Teacher

One of the goals of *Kinetic Kaleidoscope* is to give students a vocabulary so they can respond physically and verbally to the artworks they experience. The journal reinforces the new vocabulary the students are acquiring, and it gives them another avenue for translating their movements, their kinesthetic impressions, and their associated images into a different medium. The journal is also a written and visual record of the students' kinesthetic and multisensory journey in art appreciation. As they consult their journals, they can chart their own progress.

To conduct this exercise, prepare journal sheets in advance, have the students make a journal booklet, or hand out blank paper and give the students directions. Students who are familiar with visual and written journals will need little direction.

Let's Write and Draw!

♦ *You are invited to start a journal of your work in movement and art. Take your journal paper and write down anything that came to mind while you were moving and freezing during the various activities. For example, what people, activities, or places came to your mind as you explored your kinesphere?*

♦ *Select the most interesting object or activity that you found and write about it.*

♦ *Now you are invited to draw any of these objects, people, or activities.*

♦ *You can also record any feelings, images, words, or ideas that came into your mind as part of the kinesphere activities.*

Planes and Directions in Space

This section further acquaints students with diagonal, horizontal, vertical, and sagittal (front and back) planes and directions in space. These planes and directions are found in both dance and visual art. Since paintings are typically on a two-dimensional surface, depth or forward and back movement in the sagittal plane needs to be suggested through perspective, light and shadow, or color juxtapositions.

Before beginning, an important point needs to be emphasized. Artworks affect people differently. In our view there is no right way to respond to art. The process of discovering direction and other elements is a process of self-discovery. The analyses of artworks that appear in this volume reflect our responses, our way of seeing, hearing, and feeling. You may respond to the works differently. Our attitude is never that we are right and you are wrong. We encourage you to adopt the same attitude in the classroom.

We begin with diagonal influences. A good example of an art composition that is strongly diagonal is John Frederick Peto's *The Old Violin* (p. vi). The diagonal placement of the violin and the page of music are emphasized because the nearly vertical bow comes between them.

Other works are full of horizontal lines and exert a strong horizontal influence on the eye. The horizon in Francis Alexander's *Ralph Wheelock's Farm* (p. 10) exerts this kind of effect, which the clouds, rows of houses, people, and haystacks accentuate. In Eakins's *The Biglin Brothers Racing* (p. vi), other elements such as the water lines and the elongated shapes of the boats make our eyes travel horizontally across the surface. David Hockney's *Sun* (p. 10) uses both diagonal and horizontal lines.

Some artworks display a strong vertical orientation. Morris Louis's *133* (p. 10) is an example. Another good painting for illustrating vertical direction is Raoul Dufy's *Basin at Deauville* (p. 11). The masts in this painting form a series of vertical lines together with the flags arranged vertically alongside.

Movement may also be in the sagittal plane, retreating back or jumping forward. In Maurice Utrillo's *The Church at Saint-Severin* (p. 11), the eye travels from the forefront of the painting backward along the road to the human figures positioned as far back as the eye can see. The painting may even give some viewers the disturbing sensation that the eye is traveling still farther up the road, beyond the vanishing point. This sensation is produced because the lines defining the street are converging, although their point of convergence is beyond the point that the eye can go, somewhere farther up the street beyond the borders of the painting. Even though the storefront at the end of the road is diminutive in relationship to the storefront in the foreground—which suggests distance—the eye is compelled to follow the street into the background where the only human figures are placed. In the painting, the storefront is red and it frames the women, who are wearing black dresses. The contrast attracts the eye, drawing it back up the road.

In Edouard Manet's *The Races* (p. 11), the scene also seems to be retreating from us, even though, if you look closely, you will see that the horses are in fact coming toward us. The fence railings are drawn as converging diagonal lines, making the eye recede more deeply to the point of convergence, which is somewhere far back in the recesses of the painting.

The position of the horses at the back of the large, open gray space that defines the track makes the horses stand out, drawing the eye backward up the track to the place where the horses are galloping.

In Tom Neary's **By a Nose** (p. 10), the horses appear to be charging out of the painting into the foreground, directly toward the viewer. They may even give some viewers the disquieting sensation that they will break the reins of two dimensionality and run full tilt into the real world. This sensation is familiar to viewers of 3-D movies in which moving objects appear to be propelled outward, directly at the audience, which often ducks the objects they "know" can't possibly hit them.

Unlike Louis's **133** (p. 10), artworks rarely display movement in ony one direction. Multiple directional influences are usually integrated into a single painting, although one direction may dominate. Piet Mondrian's **Diamond Painting in Red, Yellow, Blue** (p. 12), which incorporates diagonal, vertical, and horizontal lines, is an especially good example. In this painting, the diamond shape of the frame establishes a tension that emphasizes the black vertical and horizontal lines forming the internal squares and rectangles. The black mass on the painting produces in some viewers a sensation of weight pulling the diamond in the direction that the black "arrow" points.

Planes and Directions Activity 1: Four Directions

To the Teacher

In the following activities students will practice translating information from one sense to another. They will find directions in artworks and express what they find in movement. They also have an opportunity to build their aesthetic vocabulary by discussing the directions they find and the movements they select to represent those directions.

You will need to find paintings, large photographs, or other works of art that are good examples of the four directions. Display the art pieces at the front of the class. Divide the class into groups of three. Students will be asked to create a sequence of three movements. Any and all combinations should be accepted and appreciated.

Let's Move!

♦ *I have put a number of different artworks in front of the class for you to see. I want each group to choose a work—or use the work I will assign to you—but don't tell the rest of the class which work you chose. First, look at the artwork. Notice the directions of the lines and the objects.*

♦ *Now, create a sequence of three movements that represent the directions you find in the painting. You can use your arms, your body, your legs, pathways on the floor, or your whole bodies. You can each perform just one of the movements at a time, one right after the other, or all three movements together . . . whichever you like.*

♦ *Now, which group is ready to share its movements? Each group can take turns showing the class. When a group is finished, we will try to guess which artwork you chose.*

Planes and Directions Activity 2: Journal

To the Teacher

Have the students take out their journals or hand out paper.

Let's Write and Draw!

♦ *Do each of you have your journals? Good. You are invited to draw lines, marks, and shapes to represent the movements you made during your "performance."*

♦ *Now, quickly draw the directions and movements one of the other groups made.*

♦ *You are invited to write how you felt as you performed your movements. What words or moods did the movements bring to mind?*

Review Activity 1: Shapes, Levels, Directions, Planes

To the Teacher

The following activity reviews the energy concepts presented in this chapter. Look for prints of works by sculptors Henry Moore and Alberto Giacometti and the painter Joan Miro. They will be good examples of shapes. Of particular interest are Miro's **Composition 1963** and **The Poetess**. Rogier van der Weyden's **St. George and the Dragon** (p. 12), Pablo Picasso's **Still Life** (p. 24), and Henri Matisse's **Beasts of the Sea** (p. 24) are other good examples.

Let's Move!

♦ *Look at the shapes these artists have created. Some of these shapes were like the ones you created with your bodies when we did the Space Shapes activity. Find a shape you like in one of these reproductions but don't tell the class which one it is.*

♦ *We will need some volunteers to come forward to make one of the shapes with their bodies. The rest of us will guess which works you are representing. We will look at the levels, shapes, directions, and planes you are using. Then we will find your shapes in one of the paintings.*

Review Activity 2: Journal

Let's Write and Draw!

♦ *Write about or draw the images that came to your mind as you explored the various shapes. You may want to combine words and drawing.*

♦ *Look at the angular and pointy shapes of the two riders in W. H. Brown's **Bareback Riders** (p. 23). How do they make you feel? Now compare Brown's pointy angular shapes with the rounded shapes of Walt Kuhn's **The White Clown** (p. 24). Describe the feelings of the clown as he waits for his turn to perform. What might be the thoughts of the bareback riders?*

♦ *Now, make a design or drawing using rounded or angular and pointy shapes. Then think of a short description to go with your design or drawing.*

Bareback Riders, 1886
W. H. Brown
National Gallery of Art, Washington, D.C.

Beasts of the Sea, 1950
Henri Matisse
National Gallery of Art, Washington, D.C.

The White Clown, 1929
Walt Kuhn
National Gallery of Art, Washington, D.C.

Still Life, 1918
Pablo Picasso
National Gallery of Art, Washington, D.C.

Self-Portrait with a Pencil, 1933
Käthe Kollwitz
National Gallery of Art, Washington, D.C.

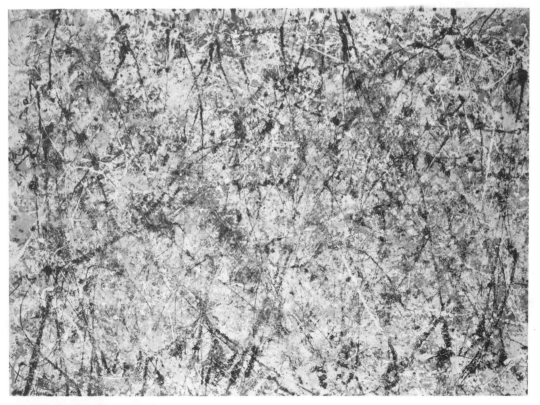

Number 1, 1950 (Lavender Mist), 1950
Jackson Pollock
National Gallery of Art, Washington, D.C.

A Lion, 1614-15
Peter Paul Rubens
National Gallery of Art, Washington, D.C.

Right and Left, 1909
Winslow Homer
National Gallery of Art, Washington, D.C.

Baby (Cradle), 1917
Gustav Klimt
National Gallery of Art, Washington, D.C.

Self-Portrait, 1889
Paul Gauguin
National Gallery of Art, Washington, D.C.

Winter Harmony, c. 1890 -1900
John Henry Twachtman
National Gallery of Art, Washington, D.C.

***Woman with a Parasol–Madame Monet
and Her Son***, 1875
Claude Monet
National Gallery of Art, Washington, D.C.

Portrait of a Lady, c. 1460
Rogier van der Weyden
National Gallery of Art, Washington, D.C.

Zirchow VII, 1918
Lyonel Feininger
National Gallery of Art, Washington, D.C.

Reconciliation Elegy, 1978
Robert Motherwell
National Gallery of Art, Washington, D.C.

Water, 1988
Leta Herman
Artist's collection

The Blank Signature, 1965
René Magritte
National Gallery of Art, Washington, D.C.

Improvisation 31 (Sea Battle), 1913
Wassily Kandinsky
National Gallery of Art, Washington, D.C.

II Laban's Four Motion Factors

Rudolf Laban made and recorded detailed observations of the energy of men and women in functional and aesthetic pursuits—for example, in dance and acting, industry, and conversation. In his three major books —*Modern Educational Dance*, *The Mastery of Movement*, and *Effort: Economy of Body Movement*, which he coauthored with F. C. Lawrence —Laban organized his observations of effort into four elemental factors of motion: time, space, force, and flow. Each motion factor can be represented as a continuum.

> A continuum is an imaginary line
> along which we can represent degrees
> of a characteristic such as color or hardness.

At the ends of each continuum lie polarities that Laban referred to as effort elements. Between these two extremes lies a range of gradations.

Each continuum can be used to represent physical, vocal, or mental energy. In human beings, energy typically requires mental and physical effort. Physical effort often has accompanying mental states or attitudes. For example, a happy frame of mind may be expressed in a jaunty gait, determination in a directed, no-nonsense walk.

In a passage in *The Mastery of Movement*, Laban stated that the creative energy of visual artists is infused and encapsulated in their creations.

> Static works of art comprise pictures, sculpture, architecturally beautiful buildings, to which we may add utilitarian objects bearing the imprint of the creative impulse of genius. In these art forms the dynamic power of the creator is enshrined in the form of his work. The movements he has used in drawing, painting, or modelling have given character to his creations, and they remain fixed in the still-visible strokes of his pencil, brush, or chisel. The activity of his mind is revealed in the form he has given to his material.(9)

Käthe Kollwitz's *Self-Portrait with a Pencil* (p. 25) is a good illustration of Laban's point. Her application of angular verticals vitalizes and charges the portrait with quick, busy energy and dynamism.

Influenced by Laban's observation, *Kinetic Kaleidoscope* adapts his movement vocabulary, modifying it as needed to describe the inner energy in the visual arts. In this chapter we discuss Laban's four Motion Factors —time, space, force, and flow—and we present activities for introducing these concepts to students.

Time

When applied to works of art, the concept of time has at least two meanings. The lines, colors, and shapes presented on the surface of a painting are the same to generations of viewers. For this reason, art is sometimes said to be timeless. In *Kinetic Kaleidoscope*, however, the concept of time has special significance. Previously we showed that the frozen surfaces of artworks contain visual aspects that cause us to feel inner movement and energy. Time is also a characteristic of this inner energy.

Energy in the time continuum ranges from sustained and leisurely to sudden and urgent.

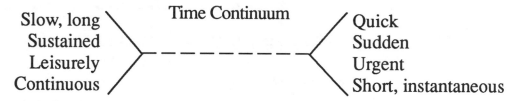

Slow, long
Sustained
Leisurely
Continuous

Time Continuum

Quick
Sudden
Urgent
Short, instantaneous

The words listed on each side of the continuum characterize the polarities of time. Although the terms in each list are not synonymous, they constitute, when taken as a group of related ideas, one or the other pole of the continuum. Movement therapist Carol Boggs aptly explains the polar elements of time in her thesis.

> The [polar] elements of quick and sustained are seen as being "attitudes" toward time. For example, according to Laban, one can experience and/or treat the passage of five minutes two different ways, either with a sense of quick urgency or with a sense of savored sustainment.

A person can treat even five minutes with quick urgency or with lingering sustainment. Even our minds may linger, for example. Mental counterparts of sustained movement are feelings of lingering, wanting something to last, and having all the time in the world. If we converse in this state, our voices might reflect a lingering quality. Think of how you talk to a friend when you are in a relaxed mood. In visual art, many aspects of a work may contribute to this feeling. Students often associate longer, continuous lines with sustained effort.

Quick or sudden movement efforts are ordinarily accompanied by a feeling of urgency or "busyness." Our minds race as we search for quick answers or solutions. Words come more rapidly, expressing to others our sense of urgency. In visual art, certain combinations of lines, shapes, or marks tend to produce in viewers a feeling of urgency, quickness, or busyness. See Jackson Pollock's *Number 1, 1950 (Lavender Mist)* (p. 25), for example.

Time Activity 1: Talking Time Drum

To the Teacher

The objective of this activity is to explore the concept of time in movement. You will need a drum. Laban's terminology is woven into the activity to familiarize students with his vocabulary.

Let's Move!

♦ *First, we are going to explore the Motion Factor of time with our kinespheres. As we move, stay within your own space bubble. Take it with you as you move to open spaces in the room. From time to time, I will talk to you as you are moving. This is called "side coaching" in acting and theater.*

♦ *Now, listen to the speed of the "talking" drum. It will tell you how fast to move. Listen carefully so that when the drum changes, your feet will follow.*

♦ [Begin to beat the drum with slow measured beats *...*...*....] *Imagine that you are walking to a certain place on a beautiful, sunny spring day. It seems you have all the time in the world. You are enjoying the sun. You want it to last. Look for the open spaces in the room. You are walking in a slow, sustained, lingering, and casual manner. . . .*

♦ *Now, become more aware of the time, of where you are going. You begin to walk a little more quickly.* [Begin to increase the speed of the drum beats *..*..*..]

♦ *Suddenly you realize you are late! You must now hurry or you'll be in big trouble. You are late, very late.* [Beat the drum very quickly, so students begin to scurry *.*.*.] *You sense the urgency of the situation.*

♦ [Then beat one loud beat after a short pause to signal stop *.] *Freeze! Now, sit in your kinesphere. Recall how you felt when you were walking slowly, in a sustained fashion. How did your body feel? How was that different from the way you felt when you had to hurry?*

Time Activity 2: Looking at Art

To the Teacher

It will be helpful for students to see color reproductions of the paintings listed below or other examples. Display the paintings at the front of the room.

If students do not know the difference between the subject or content of a painting and its formal qualities, explain the distinction to them. You might say the difference is between what the painting is about and how it is painted (for example, the use of line, shape, color, texture). A good painting for illustrating this distinction is Peter Paul Rubens's *A Lion* (p. 26). The painting's subject is the lion. Some of the formal qualities include many light, feathery, curvy lines.

Let's Look!

♦ *Look at Manet's **The Races** (p. 11), Louis's **133** (p. 10), Winslow Homer's **Right and Left** (p. 26), and Pollock's **Number 1, 1950 (Lavender Mist)** (p. 25). Look at the individual marks and strokes, shapes and lines. Which of the time energy words come to mind? Which paintings represent to you a feeling of sustained, continuous, slow energy or movement? Which represent a feeling of quick or sudden energy? Do any paintings have both qualities?*

♦ *Look at Gustav Klimt's **Baby (Cradle)** (p. 27). We can look at the painting's content (the subject of the picture or the theme) and also the painting's form (how the subject was painted—the lines, shapes, and style). In what ways do you think the painting is quick and busy? In what ways relaxed and sustained?*

Time Activity 3: Journal

To the Teacher

Although the journal activities in this section are optional, students should be encouraged to keep a journal and make entries that interest them.

Let's Draw and Write!

♦ *You are invited to draw lines and shapes or anything else to express the feelings you had when you were walking slowly.*

♦ *Now, recall how you felt when you suddenly had to hurry. How did the rhythm of your feet change? What was the pattern of your footsteps on the floor? Feel free to draw marks, lines, shapes or anything else to express your feelings.*

♦ *Can you draw lines or shapes that express each kind of time—slow and quick?*

Space

Laban's second Motion Factor is space. At one end of the space continuum, energy is direct or undeviating; on the other end, it is indirect or flexible.

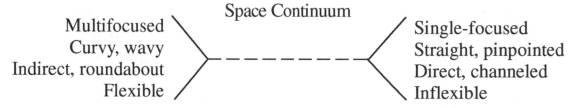

Space Continuum

Multifocused
Curvy, wavy
Indirect, roundabout
Flexible

Single-focused
Straight, pinpointed
Direct, channeled
Inflexible

Direct energy in space moves straight to a point. Mentally, direct energy can be associated with having a single focus or goal. When we are single-focused, we pay attention by channeling our energy and often by taking direct paths in space. Our minds move directly to a problem's solution and we block everything else out. Our voices can also be direct.

Indirect energy in space moves flexibly toward a point. In visual art the pathways are usually wavering. Mentally, indirect energy can be associated with having multifocused goals or spreading our attention so we can deal with many concerns at once. In this state, our minds often diverge, brainstorm, and take in more information.

Space Activity 1: Exploring the Space Continuum

To the Teacher

The objective of this activity is to help students experience the concept of space in movement and art. They will explore feelings of directness and indirectness—physically. You will need a drum.

Let's Move!

♦ *Today we are going to explore pathways in space. Find a place where you will be in a self-space and wrap your kinesphere around you. We are going to make pathways in the room. Pick a point. Focus on it. When you hear the drum sound, go to the point as directly as you can. Take the straightest route possible. Obviously, you may have to detour around people and furniture in your way, but keep focusing on your goal. Your kinesphere will shrink as you need to pass other people and objects. Ready! Go *!*

♦ [Beat the drum with one loud beat * and then use a succession of softer sounds to indicate movement.] *When you reach your point, stop.* [Use two loud beats * * to signal stop. Say "Freeze" if you need to. You can repeat the whole sequence.]

♦ *Now, pick another point in the room. This time you will take a roundabout path, going to your spot indirectly. Instead of focusing exclusively on this point while you are moving toward it, give part of your focus to other things in your path. Be open to noticing what is around you—people and things. Be multifocused. Take detours in a roundabout, flexible route, but ultimately reach your goal. Ready! Go *!* [Beat the drum again as before.]

♦ *You can move slowly or quickly. You are near your final point now. When you reach it, stop.* [Signal for the students to stop. Say "Freeze" if necessary.]

♦ *Now, relax. Can you retrace your steps in your mind's eye, back to the start of your movement? Try to retrace the pathway in your mind. Now, actually retrace your steps along the curvy path, noticing again what you noticed before, but this time in reverse order. Ready! Go *!*

Space Activity 2: Journal

Let's Draw and Write!

♦ *Your memory can use kinesthetic elements as well as visual, emotional, and aural or hearing elements. Gymnasts and other athletes, dancers, actors, and even politicians use movements to help them remember dances, postures, and words. To remember their speeches, orators of ancient Greece often practiced in their gardens or in a room to associate a specific sentence or paragraph with a particular place. Later, they would visualize the garden or room and then be able to recall the speech they wished to present. This technique is called the Method of Loci or the Location Method.*

♦ *Recall the pathways you took when you moved and sketch them.*

♦ *Recall the things—imaginary or real—that caught your interest as you moved in a curvilinear fashion. Sketch them.*

♦ *Draw a line that shows a hungry person coming home (point A) and going directly to the refrigerator to get a delicious snack (point B).*

♦ *Draw a line showing a person coming home (point A) to do a rather unpleasant chore (point B).*

♦ *Depict or write about any feelings or images that came to mind.*

Space Activity 3: Looking at Space in Art

Let's Look!

♦ *Look again at Louis's **133** (p. 10); then look at Mondrian's **Diamond Painting in Red, Yellow, Blue** (p. 12), John Henry Twachtman's **Winter Harmony** (p. 27), and Hockney's **Sun** (p. 10). Which painting do you think reveals the most flexible energy? Which reveals direct energy?*

♦ *Compare Lyonel Feininger's **Zirchow VII** (p. 28) with Paul Gauguin's **Self-Portrait** (p. 27). Which one has indirect, wavering, roundabout energy? Which one has a direct, channeled feeling?*

♦ *I would like a volunteer to come to the board and draw direct, straight energy parts or indirect, curvy parts from one of the reproductions that you see in class. Don't tell us which reproduction you are using. We will try to guess the one you have in mind.*

Space Activity 4: Journal

Let's Draw and Write!

♦ *In your journal make a box. Draw all the straight lines you see in Feininger's **Zirchow VII** (p. 28).*

♦ *Now, write about what the straight, direct lines might symbolize about Feininger's building.*

♦ *Draw another box and sketch the wavy, indirect energy you feel in Gauguin's **Self-Portrait** (p. 27).*

♦ *Write how wavy energy makes you feel.*

♦ *Write about the times you most often walk with straight, direct, single-focused energy.*

♦ *Write about the places and ways in which people move with wavering, roundabout, flexible energy.*

♦ *Draw a continuum from direct (straight) to indirect (curvy). For example, begin with a very straight line on the left side of the paper, then make the line become a little wavy, and then even more wavy until your line on the right side of the paper is very curvy.*

♦ *This time, beginning on the left, draw a shape with straight sides. Next to this first shape, draw a similar shape but make its sides a little wavy. By the time you are drawing shapes on the right, all sides of the shape should be curvy. You might imagine starting with a new cardboard box that is left in the rain and begins to lose its shape, or you may imagine something entirely different that visually changes from straight sides to curvy sides.*

♦ *Now, beginning on the left, draw marks that are extremely straight, something like short bristles on a hairbrush. As you proceed toward the right side of the paper, imagine the brush getting old and the bristles becoming slightly curved. By the time you are drawing textures on the right, they may resemble the curly coat of a lamb or something else from your imagination.*

Force

Laban referred to the Motion Factor force as "weight." Movements on one end of the force continuum are light, gentle, yielding; those on the other extreme are firm, strong, muscularly tense, and unyielding.

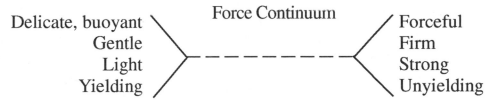

Force Continuum

Delicate, buoyant	Forceful
Gentle	Firm
Light	Strong
Yielding	Unyielding

Firm movement efforts actively use the body weight to make an impact; light movements hide one's own weight. By resisting one's own weight, one can become relatively weightless. Of course, there are many in-between states of force. Our voices and our minds also use force factors in varying degrees. Children become attuned at an early age to the subtle variations and gradations of their parents' attitudes and movement efforts.

Children know when a parent's voice is strong or firm, indicating an unyielding mind, or when it is light or gentle, indicating receptivity and openness.

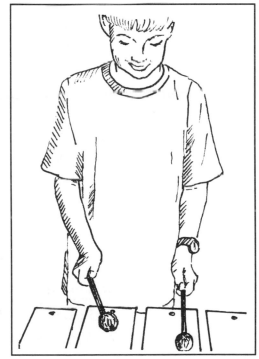

Force Activity 1: Sensing Weight

To the Teacher

The objective of this activity is to help students experience a feeling of lightness and firmness in their use of weight or force.

Let's Move!

♦ *Move into your self-space. When the drum beats, use your weight to stamp your feet in place ****. Now, create a strong pounding walk. Ready! Go!*
......*...*....* [To signal stop, beat the drum loudly twice after a brief pause in the rhythm * *.]

♦ *Stand and think about the force you use when you hammer a nail. Most of the force is located in the muscles of your arm. Think about the wood resisting the nail. If you push the nail with your hand, it resists. You will need to exert strength. Prepare to hammer the nail. Swing the hammer back over your head. Summon your strength. Feel the tension in your muscles. Now drive the hammer down on your imaginary nail, forcing it into the wood.*

♦ *Now, think about divers preparing to dive off a high diving board. They usually take a few steps forward, press hard down into the board to thrust themselves up and out. Now, get ready to mime a diver's preparatory moves. Pay attention to your muscles—the strength, firmness. Ready! Go *!*

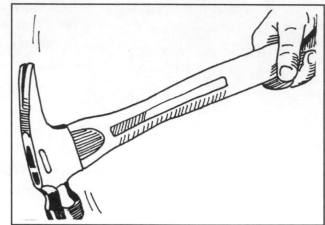

♦ *Good job! Now, picture what I am saying and mime the actions I describe as I talk. You have been given a 1-pound barbell. You are confident you can lift it, and your muscles stay relaxed as you lift it easily. It feels light so you press it up five or six times quickly. Your coach decides you are ready for a 20-pound barbell. She watches as you pick it up and press it more slowly. Now she gives you a 70-pound weight. You gather all your strength and with a tremendous effort you try to lift and press the barbell. Now, think of possible ways this scene might end. Create and mime the ending.*

♦ *Now, think about picking up a feather. Mime your thoughts. Did you notice that you did not need to exert much force?*

♦ *Think about touching a cake to see if it has risen. Mime a very light, fine touch so as not to deflate or make a dent in the cake.*

♦ *Now, walk very lightly so as not to wake your parents. Mime touching them to awaken them gently. Don't jolt or startle them.*

♦ [In the following activity you can use chimes, a lyre, or any light floating music such as Native American flute music or harp music.] *Next, you will move as though you were a helium balloon, unaffected by gravity, almost weightless, moving through space sometimes quickly, sometimes slowly. Look for the open spaces and listen to the light sound of the instrument. When the music stops, you stop. Ready! Go *! Float with your arms high in your kinesphere. And now low toward the ground. Your whole body feels lifted and light even though you are on the ground.* [Stop the music when you feel the activity is finished.]

Force Activity 2: Looking at Art

Let's Look!

- *Examine Rubens's **A Lion** (p. 26). Think about the content in terms of force. Then look at the marks that make the chalk drawing. What elements of this drawing are strong to you? Which are light? Some people might say the content or subject connotes strength while the lines used to create it are light and gentle, almost featherlike. What do you think?*

- *Look at the sky in Claude Monet's **Woman with a Parasol–Madame Monet and Her Son** (p. 28). Imagine that you have a paintbrush. How might you move your brush to create these strokes?*

- *Examine Robert Motherwell's **Reconciliation Elegy** (p. 29). Which parts are firmest, which are lightest to you?*

Force Activity 3: Journal

Let's Draw and Write!

- *Think how you felt using the firm and light movements in the activities. Recall or imagine when you had similar feelings of firmness or lightness. Think not only of physical firmness or lightness but also of mental and vocal strength or gentleness.*

- *Write about or sketch your feelings. You may want to use a combination of writing and drawing to express your ideas and feelings.*

- *Sketch or list several objects, people, animals, or environmental factors that bring firmness to mind.*

- *Try putting several of your ideas together into a picture that might be called "Maximum Firmness" or "Maximum Lightness." Or, create your own title.*

◆ *Have you ever sensed yourself in a light, airy mood or in a determined, strong, unyielding mood? Draw or describe any situation, place, or experience that comes to mind. If you wish, you may use lines, shapes, colors, or marks to graph the experience.*

◆ *Think of your morning from the time you awoke to the time you sat in class. Can you graph the energy in terms of time, space, and force? When were you lingering, hurried, directed, flexible, light, or firm? You might start at the left of the journal page and end at the right.*

Flow

Flow is the fourth and last Motion Factor. It pertains to the manner in which movement continues. Movement flow is more or less controlled or more or less free. Laban called movements on one end of the flow continuum fluent and free; he called movements at the other extreme bound, controlled, or easily stopped.

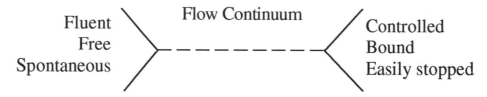

The flow continuum ranges from free to bound. Flow is a factor that accompanies other factors to some degree. We experience free flow when our movement is unobstructed. Rushing water is a metaphor from nature that explains free flow. Other metaphors may also be helpful. Free flow is experienced by dancers who once beginning a leap into the air must freely go with the flow to complete the leap safely. Trying to stop the leap in mid- air would create an awkward ending. Our movements can also be free at festive occasions when we dance with joyous spontaneity. Another good image comes from a helium balloon let loose with nothing to hold it back, free to rise and float.

The effort element of free flow can also be likened to a temper tantrum, in which a child's body parts move with little sense of where they will land. Laban called this end of the flow continuum "abandon." Here, the ability to stop is not a concern; the child is, as we say, out of control. Most often, however, we experience free flow in lesser degrees.

Although water can gush freely, it can also be controlled. For example, the boundaries of a river bank typically confine the spread of water. If a river had a will, we would say it was controlling its flow to a certain degree by building its banks and dam. A dam can block water flow completely. Our movements, too, can be planned, shaped, and controlled. We can even adjust our position at any point. Sometimes we can control our movements as precisely as a gymnast. The prize-winning gymnast must have the ability to discipline her movements, to execute them exactly as she practiced them. Or imagine a movie hero negotiating a narrow tunnel he knows to be booby trapped on all sides. He must move carefully, planting each foot cautiously, one at a time, ready to stop in mid-stream, before he plants his foot on a suspicious object. One false move would mean certain death. He dare not move freely.

In art, the Impressionists' use of light on form can help illustrate flow. Many of these painters freely merge one form into another without clear boundaries. Notice the absence of sharp boundaries in many of their works. American Impressionist Twachtman has this quality in his **Winter Harmony** (p. 27). Other artists, however, define and divide space into separate and distinct units, each having exact boundaries with a clear beginning and end. Notice the use of clear boundaries in Rogier van der Weyden's **Portrait of a Lady** (p. 28).

Flow Activity 1: Let's Flow

To the Teacher

You will need some quick and some soothing recorded music.

Let's Move!

- *Today we are going to learn about how our energy moves with free or bound flow. Move into your kinesphere.*

- *When I say "Go!" bend your knees back and forth and let all your body parts jiggle freely. Ready! Go! Jiggle like jelly!*

- *Think of a leaf now. Move freely as a leaf might travel, rolling over the ground and flying into the sky. Ready! Go!*

- [Use any music you like.] *Now, listen to the music and dance freely in any way you like within your kinesphere. When the music stops, you stop. Ready! Go!* [Wait a few moments.] *Stop! When you were enjoying the movement, you did not think about stopping. That is free flow. When you heard me say "Stop," you had to bind your movement. Some of your muscles had to tighten so that you could stop. That is bound flow. You controlled your body more when you had to stop.*

♦ *Now, we will do the activity again with different kinds of music.* [Use a different kind of music.] *Dance freely. When the music stops, freeze and make a bound statue. Make it a strange shape. Ready! Go!*

♦ *Now, think about how you would carry a very expensive $2,000 vase to its special table in your home. You might imagine yourself looking carefully at the path you take so as not to bump against any furniture. Now mime the movements. Ready! Go!*

♦ *Good. That was bound flow movement. Now, how would you carry a tea cup and saucer to a queen or very important person visiting your home? Now, everyone mime the movement. Ready! Go!*

♦ *Now, mime as I speak. Look at another person's desk in the room, pick up your cup and saucer, and walk to the desk. The cup is filled to the brim. Don't spill a drop! Control your movement so that you can stop at any point. Finally, put the saucer down carefully. Good!*

♦ *Some people can walk on sharp stones by controlling the muscles in their feet so that they do not exert pressure when they feel especially pointy stones. Now, imagine you are barefoot. You have to walk across sharp stones. You put your foot down and the stones hurt. Now, walk carefully to keep from putting weight on the sharp stones. Ready! Go!*

Flow Activity 2: Moving in Moon Space

To the Teacher

This activity emphasizes control. As students attempt to lift their legs high to mime weightlessness on the moon, they must also control their movements to maintain their balance. Use any slow, electronic space music or a xylophone, lyre, or chimes.

Let's Move!

♦ *Another type of movement that is bound is the slow space walk. Imagine you are a traveler in space and have landed on the moon. You open the hatch and descend. Walk as though you were on the moon and weightless. Ready! Go!*

◆ *Your body rises slooowly and sinks slooowly. Your knees rise higher on the moon than on the earth. So do your feet. A little effort goes a long way, so you need to maintain your balance. Maintaining your balance requires some bound flow.*

◆ *Now, freeze in the middle of your movement. Good! Some of you even froze your shape with your leg up in the air. The space walk is very controlled here on Earth so we can keep our balance.*

Flow Activity 3: Looking at Art

Let's Look!

◆ *Look at Leta Herman's **Water** (p. 29) and Neal Parks's **Oil Pastel** (cover). Although parts of both might be considered light in touch, what feeling do you experience in terms of flow? Which is freer? Which has clearer boundaries? Are there any free-flow aspects to Parks's painting?*

◆ *Examine Feininger's **Zirchow VII** (p. 28) and Pollock's **Number 1, 1950 (Lavender Mist)** (p. 25). In which do you feel a sense of abandon and spontaneity, in which a feeling of control? In which do you feel free and unbound energy? Which are bound at the edges of shapes by distinct lines or separations?*

◆ *Look at René Magritte's **The Blank Signature** (p. 30), Weyden's **Portrait of a Lady** (p. 28), and Wassily Kandinsky's **Improvisation 31 (Sea Battle)** (p. 30). Which paintings have bound forms in your opinion? Which have fluent or free parts?*

Flow Activity 4: Journal

Let's Draw and Write!

◆ *Recall a time when you felt spontaneous and free in your movements or mental attitude. Depict this feeling with words, marks and lines, or specific images.*

◆ *Recall a time when you felt bound or when you were able to control your every move. Depict this feeling, place, or situation with shapes, forms, lines, or words.*

Gesture Drawing

♦ *Create a gesture drawing. A gesture drawing is a free-flow sketch with light, circular, overlapping lines completed in about 20 or 30 seconds. A gesture drawing has little detail; it is a sketch of the general overall shape of a figure. Before you begin, copy the illustration of a gesture drawing just to get the feel of how the lines move.*

♦ *Now, try making your own gesture drawings. Remember, you should spend only 20 or 30 seconds on each drawing. Your arm does not rest on the page but is free to move as your hand moves in quick, circular motions.*

♦ *On the left side of a journal page, do a gesture drawing of yourself in an angular, jagged shape.*

♦ *On the right side of the page, do a gesture drawing of yourself in a smooth, rounded shape.*

Review Activity 1: Energy Words

To the Teacher

Ask students for definitions of energy and briefly discuss the ones they give you. Next, ask students to describe the kind of energy they see in several contrasting paintings that you place before them. They may use words such as "busy," "wild," "lots of dots," "jagged lines," "smooth shapes," "wispy textures," "heavy shapes," "jumpy marks." If they say only one word in noun form ("shapes," for example) ask, "What kind?"

Next, categorize these words into Laban's four Motion Factors. For example:

Time	Space	Weight/Force	Flow
Busy	Jagged Lines	Wispy Textures	Wild Colors
Lots of Dots	Smooth Shapes	Heavy Shapes	Hazy Shapes
Long Lines	Curvy	Strong Shapes	Filmy
Short Lines	Straight Lines	Thick, Dark Lines	
Jumpy Marks			

Let's Talk!

♦ *Brainstorm words that describe the movement and energy you see in the various works of art before you. Try to remember the movement vocabulary we discussed but don't limit yourself to those terms. Think of words that describe the type of movement and energy you see. There are no "right" or "correct" answers, just many ideas and feelings. I will write the words on the board as you give them to me.* [Write all their responses.]

♦ *Now, let's review the Motion Factors. I will write them on the board as you tell them to me.* [Time, space, force, flow.]

♦ *Now, let's put our descriptive words in one or more of the categories: time, space, force, flow.* [As the students talk about the energy they see in the works of art, place their words under a category. Some words fit under several categories.]

♦ *Now, choose a word and make movements like the word. Ready. Go!*

Review Activity 2: Journal

Let's Write!

♦ *With a partner (or by yourself), list at least ten words that describe the energy you see in the lines, colors, shapes, and textures in Picasso's **Still Life** (p. 24).*

♦ *Now, place those words in the most appropriate Motion Factor category— time, space, force, flow.*

Cattleya Orchid and Three Brazilian Hummingbirds, 1871
Martin Heade
National Gallery of Art, Washington, D.C.

A View of Salisbury Cathedral, c. 1825
John Constable
National Gallery of Art, Washington, D.C.

Still Life with Sleeping Woman, 1940
Henri Matisse
National Gallery of Art, Washington, D.C.

The Lighthouse at Honfleur, 1886
Georges Seurat
National Gallery of Art, Washington, D.C.

Woman in a Striped Dress, 1895
Edouard Vuillard
National Gallery of Art, Washington, D.C.

The Aero, c. 1914
Marsden Hartley
National Gallery of Art, Washington, D.C.

Siegfried and the Rhine Maidens, 1888-91
Albert Pinkham Ryder
National Gallery of Art, Washington, D.C.

III Eight Effort Actions

The activities in this section will acquaint students with Laban's eight Effort Actions. They are combinations of the elements found in the Motion Factors—time, space, and weight (force). Flow, the fourth Motion Factor, with its extreme elements—free to bound—is not used in the definition of Effort Actions because each action may be either free or bound. For example, pressing tends to be bound, but it can be free at another time. Floating tends to be free, but it can also be bound.

The Effort Actions are types of movement. Somewhat akin to stereotypes, their extreme characteristics are hard to find in reality. However, familiarity with Laban's Effort Actions is useful for understanding our kinesthetic responses to the visual arts. The following chart enumerates the eight Effort Actions and the corresponding Motion Factors—time, space, force.

Effort Action	Time	Space	Force
Float	Sustained	Indirect	Light
Glide	Sustained	Direct	Light
Dab	Quick	Direct	Light
Flick	Quick	Indirect	Light
Wring	Sustained	Indirect	Firm
Press	Sustained	Direct	Firm
Punch	Quick	Direct	Firm
Slash	Quick	Indirect	Firm

In the following activities students will first experience the light Effort Actions and then the firm. They will simulate the Effort Actions in speech and movement. The purpose of the activities is to facilitate a kinesthetic response to styles of art, to particular artworks, and to parts of works. It is not an attempt to match the words exactly with what the teacher might believe is the "correct" answer. When a student identifies an unexpected Effort Action (for example, a "dab") to describe a work, the teacher might ask, "What part of the painting dabs for you? Why?" Then the teacher might say, "Oh, now I see why you used that word. What does someone else feel?" For all these activities, it is important to remind students that they are safe to express their ideas and kinesthetic responses.

We will now explore the four light Effort Actions. Float will be the first.

Float Activity 1: Hello

To the Teacher

A float is sustained, indirect, and light.

Let's Move!

♦ *Today we are going to learn about Effort Actions. The first Effort Action is float. Find a space where your kinesphere will not touch anyone else's.* [This activity can also be performed with arms only, with students in their seats.]

♦ *Lift your arms over your head and float them lightly like a balloon or cloud. Let them sink and rise in space in a curving fashion, up and down and all around.*

♦ *Now, use your voice to mirror the rise and fall and curves of your floating arms. Say,*

"Helllll...oooooooo. Hoooooooow aaaaare yooooou tooooodaaaaaay?"

♦ *On an oscilloscope, a screen that traces speech patterns electronically, your voice might look like this:*

♦ *What characters might move or sound like that?* [Answers can range from birds and snobby people to jellyfish and singers.]

Float Activity 2: Looking at Art

Let's Look!

♦ *An example of an artwork that has some light, flexible, sustained floating qualities is Martin Heade's* **Cattleya Orchid and Three Brazilian Hummingbirds** *(p. 48). Notice the light and free quality of the air and the general feeling of quietness in the landscape. Most of the shapes are soft curves, which provide an indirect quality to the artwork. The whole top half of the painting seems almost to float off the canvas.*

Glide Activity 1: Hello

To the Teacher

A glide is sustained, direct, and light.

Let's Move!

♦ *Glide is the second Effort Action we will explore. Lift one arm lightly. Glide it very slowly on one level directly away from your body in a straight-lined path. The movement might feel somewhat like the continuous, even glide of an ice skater.*

♦ *Now, do the movement again and use your voice to mirror the straight, slow, lightness of your movement. Say,*

"Helllll...oooooooo. Hooooooow aaaaare yooooou tooooodaaaaaay?"

♦ *How many pitches did you hear? [One.] The one pitch you heard throughout is called a monotone, and on a voice screen it would look like a thin gliding arm. Let me draw a one-pitch gliding voice on the board. Each word is spoken in the same tone and is drawn out in a line like this:*

♦ *What characters might move or sound like that? [Answers range from ghosts and Glenda the Good Witch to skaters and hawks.]*

Glide Activity 2: Looking at Art

Let's Look!

♦ *Look at Alexander's **Ralph Wheelock's Farm** (p. 10). Does any part seem to glide—lightly, directly, and continuously—in the painting?*

♦ *In John Constable's **A View of Salisbury Cathedral** (p. 48), our eyes might glide over the grass, then move vertically to the church spire and float in the sky.*

Dab Activity 1: Hello

To the Teacher

A dab is quick, direct, and light. You will need a tone block. For the mime activity you can have several percussion instruments available for sound effects although students can use their voices, also.

Let's Move!

♦ *The dab is the third Effort Action. Bend your elbows and dab your fingers as though you were typing on a typewriter or computer. Your machine is quite sensitive to your touch so you need only to touch it lightly. Are your movements quick or sustained? Your fingers will go directly and quickly to the keys. Now, dab with your noses as I tap the tone block***. Dab with your hips. Dab with your shoulders. Dab with your feet.*

♦ *Now, let's use our voices to match our movements as we dab with our finger. Say,*

> *"Hell.o. How.are.you.to.day? How.are.you.to.day?"*

You used a quick, light, staccato monotone. I can represent dabbing with repetitive dots or brief, short pats and taps.

● ●

♦ *What things can you imagine that would make that kind of movement and sound?* [Answers range from chipmunks and rabbits to chickens and robots.]

Dab Activity 2: Mime

Let's Move!

♦ *Find a partner.*

♦ *Brainstorm machines and activities that make tapping noises like a person using a Morse Code machine, a typewriter, or a computer. Think of other activities or objects that make tapping noises. Now, choose one.*

♦ *Decide who will be the mime in this activity. Your partner will make the sound effects. The person making the sounds needs to watch the mime very carefully so the sounds fit the movements. Now, decide on a beginning and ending tableau. A tableau is a frozen shape a mime can make.*

♦ *All the mimes make their tableau, hold it for the count of five to give us a clear beginning, and perform the mime with sounds from the sound effects person. Ready. Go!* [Appreciate their efforts. If a couple is willing to share their mime with everyone else, encourage them.]

Dab Activity 3: Looking at Art

♦ *Notice the light, quick, direct dabs in* **The Lighthouse at Honfleur** *(p. 49) by Georges Seurat. The whole painting consists of light, quick, direct points. Do you see any dabs in Henri Matisse's* **Still Life with Sleeping Woman** *(p. 49) or Edouard Vuillard's* **Woman in a Striped Dress** *(p. 50)?*

Flick Activity 1: Hello

To the Teacher

A flick is quick, indirect, and light.

Let's Move!

♦ *The flick is the fourth Effort Action. Try to flick a speck off your sleeve. Your fingers or the back of your hand moves down, up, down, up, down, up.*

♦ *Now, flick with other body parts—your nose, your elbow, your hips, your shoulders. Remember a flick is curved, a dab is direct.*

♦ *If I make flicking marks on the board, they can look like this:*

♦ *Now, let's make our voices match as we say "Hello." Say,*

"Hell. How you day?"

♦ *What characters sound like that?* [Answers range from mice and birds to nervous people.]

Flick Activity 2: Looking at Art

Let's Look!

♦ *Now look at a painting. A flick is different from a dab in that a flick has a curving or indirect quality about it. In Monet's **Woman with a Parasol–Madame Monet and Her Son** (p. 28), do you see any light, curving, quick flicks or any direct, light dabs? Where?*

Flick Activity 3: Moving with Art

To the Teacher

In this activity, it might be difficult for students to guess which reproduction their classmates are interpreting kinetically. Correctness is not essential. The kinetic response is the important part! An alternative to guessing is to ask the movers to tell which painting they chose to interpret with movement. You may substitute other paintings if you like.

Let's Move!

♦ *Look at the following paintings: Seurat's **The Lighthouse at Honfleur** (p. 49), Twachtman's **Winter Harmony** (p. 27), Matisse's **Still Life with Sleeping Woman** (p. 40), Rubens's **A Lion** (p. 26), and Monet's **Woman with a Parasol–Madame Monet and Her Son** (p. 28).*

♦ *With your bodies in your own kinesphere, pick one painting to represent by moving your body. You can choose any part of the painting or the feeling you have for the whole painting. Do the movement over and over with any body part. Begin when I beat the drum. Ready! Go *!*

♦ *Now, we will guess which painting you used. Who wants to show his or her movement first?*

Wring Activity 1: Hello

To the Teacher

Now we will examine the four firm Effort Actions. The sensation of firmness includes the relationship of the body's mass to gravity—actively moving through it, creating forceful, strong movement. The first firm Effort Action will be the wring. It is sustained, indirect, and firm. If we apply more of our weight or actively use our muscles, we can turn a float into a wringing, twisting movement.

Let's Move!

♦ *Let's move our hands and arms firmly and slowly, in a curved manner, as if we are wringing out a towel.*

♦ *We can wring with our whole body, too, in a twisting motion while keeping our feet on the center spot. Ready! Go!*

♦ *This is how a wring might look on paper. The thick lines show the firmness.*

♦ *Now, let's speak with a wringing, twisting voice as we do the movements. Say,*

> *"Helllll...ooooooo.*
> *Hooooooow aaaaare*
> *yooooou*
> *tooooodaaaaaay?"*

♦ *What characters sound or move like that?* [Answers usually range from witches to complainers.]

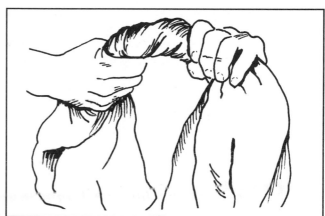

Wring Activity 2:   Looking at Art

Let's Look!

♦ *Look at Albert Pinkham Ryder's **Siegfried and the Rhine Maidens** (p. 50). What do you sense in this painting? Is it direct and straight or indirect and flexible? Is it firm or light? Is it sustained and slow or sudden and quick? What parts give you a feeling of wringing and twisting?*

Press Activity 1: Hello

To the Teacher

A press is sustained, direct, and firm.

Let's Move!

♦ *When we change the lightness of a glide into firmness, we perform a press. A press is like a benchpress—firm, direct, slow. Think of pushing a large box before you.*

♦ *Move your hands in front of you with a slow, steady, firm, direct motion, like this:*

♦ *Now, use your voice in the same monotone manner as in the glide, but give it more intensity as you do the pressing movement Say,*

> *"Helllll...ooooooo. Hooooooow aaaaare yooooou tooooodaaaaaay?"*

♦ *What characters, animals, or objects might move or sound like that?* [Answers may range from a steamroller to a computerized voice.]

Press Activity 2: Looking at Art

Let's Look!

♦ *Look at Louis's **133** (p. 10). Some people might sense a continuous, direct firmness in the lines. What do you feel?*

♦ *Can you find a press in any of the paintings we have seen so far?*

Punch Activity 1: Hello

To the Teacher

A punch is quick, direct, and firm. When we add power to a dab, we perform a punch or thrust into space. A punch is usually longer than a dab because it is firmer. In visual art a punch has more mass, density, and width. The light efforts, on the other hand, are often transparent or translucent; the firm efforts are usually opaque, dark, or intense. A drum will help in this activity.

Let's Move!

♦ *Find your own self-space.*

♦ *Move your arms suddenly and forcefully in a direct punch or thrust. [Beat the drum to encourage punching or thrusting movements. Be sure all the students are in their own spaces.] Ready! Go***! Try pounding into the floor with your feet. Ready! Go***!*

♦ *Now, punch the air in your kinesphere with your elbows. Listen to the drum. It tells you when to stop. Ready! Go***! [To signal stop, beat the drum once loudly after a brief pause.]*

♦ *Now, let's speak in a punching voice as we do the movements. Say,*

    "Hell.o. How. are. you. to. day?"

♦ *I will draw three or four firm, thick, straight lines to show punching.*

▬▬▬ ▬▬▬ ▬▬▬ ▬▬▬

♦ *The punching lines are longer and thicker than a dab because they are stronger and go farther. The sudden punching line is shorter than the long, slow press.*

Punch Activity 2: Looking at Art

Let's Look!

♦ *A punch is firm, direct, and quick. Do you see any punches in Marsden Hartley's* **The Aero** *(p. 50)? Some people sense punches in the strong, straight white lines and short black lines. Others see the big red shape as a big punch.*

Slash Activity 1: Hello

To the Teacher

A slash is quick, indirect, and firm. If we add strength and power to a flick, we are likely to perform a slash with our whole arm.

Let's Move!

- *Place your hand high over your head, out to the same side as your arm. Now quickly and strongly slash your hand and arm down across the front of your body on a diagonal, curved pathway to the other side of your body. Imagine you are slashing your way through the brush of a thick forest.*

- *When I draw slashing lines, they are firm, curved, and quick, like this:*

- *Use your voice in a slashing manner to mirror slashing movements. Say,*

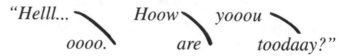

"Helll...   *Hoow*   *yooou*

oooo.   *are*   *toodaay?"*

Slash Activity 2: Looking at Art

Let's Look!

- *Look at Thomas Chambers's* **Felucca off Gibraltar** *(p. 68) and* **The Aero** *(p. 50) by Hartley. What lines or shapes give you a feeling of strength and firmness? Do you see any slashing ones? Are they direct or indirect and flexible?*

- *Look at Dufy's* **Basin at Deauville** *(p. 11) and Homer's* **Right and Left** *(p. 26). Describe the Effort Actions you see in these paintings.*

- *A slash is quick, curved, and firm. Look at the way the foliage in Henri Rousseau's* **The Equatorial Jungle** *(p. 69) makes many quick, curved shapes. Some people say the foliage looks like slashing claw marks. What do you feel about the painting? Do you feel other Effort Actions, too?*

Effort Action Review Activities

Review Activity 1: Contrasting Artwork

Let's Write!

♦ *Now that you have become familiar with the eight basic Effort Actions, you can view contrasting artworks and describe them using your new terminology. You may use the two examples that follow or find other examples in library books.*

♦ *Look at Matisse's **Still Life with Sleeping Woman** (p. 49). Use your brainstorming skills to list as many single words as you can to describe the movement and energy you see in this work.*

♦ *Now, contrast Matisse's work with another picture of a table and plants—Henri Fantin-Latour's **Still Life** (p. 69). Here is a work that is much more bound and controlled. Again, list words to describe the energy and movement you see and feel in this artwork.*

Review Activity 2: Robot

To the Teacher

The objective of the following activity is to help the students become more familiar with the combination of lightness and dabbing. Decide upon an area for students to move within. They will need to do some reaching in their kinespheres. You will need a woodblock, tone block, or other percussion instrument that has a quick, light sound. Look at the quick, direct dabs of Seurat's **The Lighthouse at Honfleur** (p. 49). They resemble the light, quick sounds you will be making with the instruments.

Let's Move!

♦ *Find an open space for your kinesphere where you can stretch without bumping into anyone or anything. Today we are going to experience the quick, light movement of the dab. The activity is called the "Robot" and some of you might feel like a robot as you move; others will be reminded of other things.* [Responses might include dabbing medicine on a cut or blotting lipstick.]

♦ *When you hear the taps of the instrument, dab one part of your body quickly and lightly. Choose one part only, such as your head, forearm,* *hand, or knee. As you hear the taps, move your body so that the movement ends almost as quickly as the sound. Ready! Go***!*

♦ *Now, choose a different body part. Dab it when you hear the instrument. Ready! Go***!*

♦ *Now, choose several body parts. Dab one several times, then move the other while keeping the first still. Every so often change focus by moving just your head in a new direction. Then, move your whole body in a pivot toward that new direction. Some of you might feel like moving robots. Ready! Go***!*

♦ *Now, dab with your nose, like this.* [Demonstrate for the students by dabbing with your nose and walking in little dabbing steps. Say the White Rabbit's words, "I'm late, I'm late, for a very important date. No time to say hello, good-bye. I'm late, I'm late, I'm late."] *Now, you try.*

♦ *Now, dab with your foot. Dab lightly and quickly with your elbow. What did that feel like? What characters might move like that?* [Answers might range from rabbits and mice to a variety of other characters.]

♦ *One of the most famous artists who used this type of movement in his paintings was Georges Seurat. This style of painting with dabs is called* pointillism *because Seurat made his paintings by dabbing on little points of paint.*

♦ *One example of Seurat's pointillism is* **The Lighthouse at Honfleur** *(p. 49). Even though Seurat's dabs are light and quick, they are controlled. Each dab makes a point so that we know where one point ends and another begins. Yet overall, the shapes sometimes meld freely one into the other leaving no clear boundaries.*

Review Activity 3: Flick a Fly

Let's Move!

♦ *Another quick, light movement is called a flick. With your finger, try flicking an imaginary fly off your arm, hand, nose, and head.*

♦ *Now, try flicking the same annoying fly with your hand. Try to get it off your shoulder, your elbow, and your knee. Now, imagine that your arms are full of books and you are in a hurry to class. You now must flick the fly with your head.*

◆ *Some animals and characters flit and flick. Sometimes a horse shivers its muscles to flick a fly. Some lines in paintings are also little flicks. Pick a flicking animal to depict with you body. Ready! Go!*

Review Activity 4: Looking at Art

Let's Look!

◆ *Can you find some dabs and flicks in Pollock's **Number 1, 1950 (Lavender Mist)** (p. 25) and Vuillard's **Woman in a Striped Dress** (p. 50)?*

Review Activity 5: Interpreting Art with Music

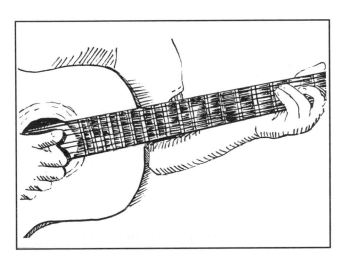

To the Teacher

The purpose of this activity is to help students relate their movement   vocabulary to artwork. You will need a variety of percussion and, if possible, stringed instruments for the students to use as they transform energy in painting to energy in sound. You might also want to ask students to find paintings that show the different Effort Actions. These might be their own or ones they find elsewhere in books or on school walls.

Suggested instruments

- Drums for firmness: hand drum, bongos, log drum, slit drum, steel drum
- Wooden instruments for quickness: tone block, woodblock, rhythm   sticks, temple block, claves
- Gongs for sustained, direct (monotone), gliding or pressing sounds: gong, finger cymbals, cymbals
- Stringed instruments for lightness: dulcimer, lap lyre, guitar, banjo, violin, cello, autoharp, zither
- Metal instruments for lightness and sustained or quick sounds: chimes, xylophone, glockenspeil, thumb piano. (A glisando makes a sustained sound; a strike makes a light quick sound.)

Let's Move!

♦ *Look at all these works of art and all these musical instruments! Listen to the sounds of several of the instruments.* [Demonstrate their sound qualities by playing them.]

♦ *Who can find a part of a painting that might sound like one of these sounds?* [Play an instrument. Then call on a student to tell which reproduction might have the same quality visually.]

♦ *Good. Who can find another part of a painting that might be interpreted with one of the sounds you heard?*

♦ *Now, I need volunteers to interpret reproductions. Choose an instrument and stand near the reproduction you wish to interpret.* [Call on as many as there are instruments.] *Now, when I call your name, play the instrument and tell why you chose that particular instrument for that painting.* [Students might respond by naming Motion Factor elements such as lightness, strength, sustained or long lines, and so forth. Or they might name an Effort Action such as a dab to go with a tone block, a press or glide for a gong, a float for a stringed instrument. They might also use levels and directions. We are always surprised how easily they can make connections between sounds and visual aspects.]

Review Activity 6: Journal

To the Teacher

The following activities are options for students. Encourage them to create their own problems to solve, also.

Let's Draw and Write!

♦ *With a pencil, oil pastels, crayons, pastels, paint, pen, or other marker, create an effort picture. Choose one or two efforts. Use any marks, shapes, or realistic images you like.*

♦ *Use a pencil or marker to draw a flicking motion. Then use this type of movement to write your name using flicks. Now, write your name using only dabbing motions. Which style of your name do you like better, the one made with dabs or the one with flicks? Why?*

♦ *Write about the differences between two efforts, such as the dab and the flick, the press and the glide, or the wring and the punch. What does each bring to mind? What Motion Factors do each possess?*

♦ *Do you know any characters from T.V. or novels you've read that might represent one of the Effort Actions? Tell why.*

♦ *Can you create an effort dance on paper? Think of a song and make lines or shapes that represent the efforts you feel. When does it dab or feel quick and light? Is it ever strong and loud? Is it ever sustained and slow? You can create the lines and ask a friend to tell you which movement efforts come to mind. Your friend will be "reading and interpreting" your visual energy.* [Give students a chance to have their friends interpret their effort drawings.]

Review Activity 7: Explosive Shapes and Melting Shapes

To the Teacher

The objective of this activity is to help students feel the effort elements of firmness and lightness in the Motion Factor Laban called "weight." Firmness can be found in four Effort Actions: punching, pressing, wringing, and slashing. Lightness can be found in floating, gliding, flicking, and dabbing.

Let's Move!

♦ *First, we will explore the element of firmness in movement. You will first be punching or exploding into a shape.*

♦ *Stand and find your kinesphere. When the drum sounds, explode into a shape and then freeze. You do not have to know what the shape will be. You can improvise. Ready! Go *! Stop!*

♦ *Good. You were able to freeze and hold your shapes. That means you have some control of your space and your flow of movement.*

♦ *Now, when the drum sounds, explode again, quickly and firmly into another shape on a different level. If you last had a low shape close to* *the floor, try moving to a high level. Use your muscles to make your shape tight. Ready! Go *!*

♦ *Good. Now, hold that shape and when you hear the drum, move into another shape. Ready! Go *!*

♦ *Notice what images come to mind as you take one shape or another. Ready! Go *!*

♦ *Hold the last shape. When I come to tap you on the shoulder, tell me what image came to mind.* [Let several students share their images.]

♦ *Now, we will explore the element of lightness. You will use floating and gliding efforts to "melt" into a shape. In your kinespheres listen to the sounds of the xylophone* [or chimes, or lyre] *and float into and out of curvy positions. When the xylophone makes one very loud sound and pauses, lightly hold your shape right where it is. Ready! Go *!* [Sound the instrument.]

♦ *Good. Next time be sure to change levels and directions. Ready! Go *! Again. Ready! Go *!*

♦ *Good. Now use a gliding effort to melt into your final shape.*

♦ *Good. What images came to mind? I'll tap you and you tell what image you had. Keep your shape.*

Review Activity 8: Explosive Shapes with a Partner

To the Teacher

The objective of this activity is to give students practice in responding to a partner with whole body firmness and quickness (punching and slashing). You will need a drum.

Let's Move!

♦ *Find a partner.*

♦ *When the drum sounds, one of you (A) will move swiftly and firmly into a strong shape. Then, almost immediately, the drum will sound again. The second person (B) will follow making another swift, firm shape on another level. You might choose to mirror A's first shape, or you might choose to complement it by making one of your own. In dance and theater this is called a movement energy conversation. All the A's raise a hand. All the B's raise a hand. Good. You will know who you are when I call A or B.*

- *A's start. Ready! Go *!*
- *B's answer with a shape. Ready. Go *!*
- *[Continue beating the drum several more times. Then B's can go first.]*

Review Activity 9: Wring and Press

To the Teacher

Ravi Shankar's music from India is excellent for pressing and wringing actions. You will also need a drum.

Let's Move!

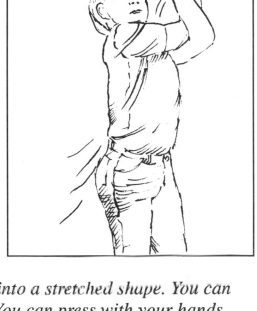

- *When I beat the drum, slowly with even beats, move around slowly and firmly in your space as though you were wringing your body. Keep one foot on a center spot in your kinesphere. Ready! Go *!*

- *Notice what images come to mind.*

- *Now, firmly and slowly press straight into a stretched shape. You can actually think of pressing something. You can press with your hands, your back, your legs, or other parts of your body. When you hear the drum again, freeze your shape firmly. Ready! Go *!*

- *Now, press into a different level using a diagonal. Remember, diagonals cross over from one side to another as well as change levels.*

To the Teacher

Form one circle or several circles of 6-10 students. Each circle will become a group kinesphere.

Let's Move!

◆ *When you hear the drum, one person at a time will press or wring his or her body in the group's kinesphere for four counts. On the fourth count, that person will freeze in a shape. Then the next person will press or wring and then freeze on the fourth count and so on around the group. Let's begin counting out loud softly. This group will demonstrate first. Ready! Go ****! ****!*

◆ *Good. Now, all the groups move to the music—one person at a time—using the firm efforts of pressing and wringing to the count of four. Ready! Go ****!*

Felucca off Gibraltar, mid-19th century
Thomas Chambers
National Gallery of Art, Washington, D.C.

The Equatorial Jungle, 1909
Henri Rousseau
National Gallery of Art, Washington, D.C.

Still Life, 1866
Henri Fantin-Latour
National Gallery of Art, Washington D.C.

Kitchen III, c. 1978
Ann Rosebrooks
National Gallery of Art, Washington, D.C.

Still Life, c. 1900
Paul Cézanne
National Gallery of Art, Washington, D.C.

IV Kinetic Energy in the Arts Activities

In the preceding chapters, *Kinetic Kaleidoscope* focused on building a vocabulary related to kinetic energy. We concentrated on analysis, breaking down movement energy into four Motion Factors and eight Effort Actions. The purpose was to introduce students to the energy in artworks and to give them a vocabulary for describing artworks and expressing their own responses. This work was preparatory. Most art incorporates diverse elements into an integrated whole. The activities in this chapter help students experience, identify, discuss, and manipulate movement elements they find integrated into a single work of art. Many of the activities also involve translating the energy in artworks from the visual into other senses to expand students' appreciation and reinforce their recollection. This translation is called *synesthesia*. With it we can "sing" colors, "draw" sounds, and "dance" lines.

Motion Factors

Kinetic Energy Activity 1: A Moveable Feast

To the Teacher

This activity will review the energy vocabulary. The movable feast refers to the festive and kinetic appreciation of art. Although students may respond verbally, these activities will expand their reactions by encouraging and developing kinetic responses. Consequently, students come to know works of art in a new way.

For this activity you will need to select at least 6–10 art reproductions. Display them in front of the class and leave them there for subsequent activities.

Let's Move!

♦ *Look at all the reproductions for parts that emphasize lightness, quickness, firmness, sustainment, directness, flexibility, freedom, or control.*

♦ *Now, find the reproduction you want to use, but don't tell anyone what it is. Next, think about which Motion Factor your artwork emphasizes. Remember, your opinion is more important than a "correct" answer. For example, what you feel is firm or light in an artwork is your opinion.*

- *Do you feel your reproduction has quick or sustained energy? If so, what is the Motion Factor? Yes, time is correct.*

- *Do you feel your reproduction has light or firm energy? If so, what is the Motion Factor? Yes, force.*

- *Do you feel your reproduction has direct, straight, single-focused or indirect, curvy, multifocused energy? If so, what is the Motion Factor? Space, good.*

- *Do you feel your reproduction is tight and controlled or free and spontaneous? If so, what is the Motion Factor? Flow is correct.*

- *Your willingness to participate and think creatively during these activities is important. What is valued is your opinion.*

Effort Actions

Kinetic Energy Activity 2: Interpreting Art

Let's Move!

- *Now, pick a section of the art reproduction that you can interpret with an Effort Action. Find an Effort Action—float, glide, flick, dab, punch, press, slash, or wring—that you see in the artwork you selected. Now, make movements that you think fit that Effort Action. Ready! Go!*

- *Who would like to volunteer to do a movement for the class? We will guess which artwork you are interpreting. Several of you will get a chance to volunteer.*

- *Next, I will invite other volunteers to interpret part of their artwork. We will try to guess which artwork is being interpreted.*

Kinetic Energy Activity 3: Journal

Let's Draw!

♦ *In the squares below draw the extremes of the Motion Factors:*

Time	Space	Force	Flow
slow	curvy	light	free
quick	straight	firm	bound

♦ *In the squares below make a drawing of each of the eight Effort Actions:*

float	glide	flick	dab
punch	slash	wring	press

♦ *Combine any of the above drawings to express how you feel when going to a new school for the first time. Make a title for your drawing. Can you tell a story about it?*

Kinetic Kaleidoscope © 1992 Zephyr Press, Tucson, AZ

Efforts and Sounds

Kinetic Energy Activity 4: Conductor

To the Teacher

Select one student to be the first conductor. Then let several other students have turns being the conductor.

Let's Move!

♦ *I would like to have a volunteer go to the front of the class. Our volunteer will stand in front of us and move with direct pressing or gliding. The rest of us will respond to the conductor by making one sustained sound that each of us has chosen. Use any vowel sound you wish, for example, a, e, i, o, u, oo, ow, or ah. When the conductor uses strength, our voices will respond with strength, becoming louder or more intense. If the conductor uses lightness, we will respond with a softer, lighter vocal quality. When the conductor freezes, we will stop. We will need to watch our conductor closely. Ready! Go!*

♦ *Now the conductor will move with sudden dabbing or punching movements and we will make dabbing and punching sounds. We will respond to dabbing with quick, light, direct single notes. Consonant sounds work well for dabbing. Punching sounds will be quick, direct, and firm. Our conductor will show us when to stop and go by alternating between moving and freezing. Our conductor will need to be very obvious when freezing so that we will know when to stop making sounds.*

♦ *This time the conductor will use a combination of gliding and flicking. Flicking sounds are quick and light, but they have more than one tone. Flicking sounds can be made by raising or lowering the pitch on the end of the sound. They are flexible and indirect, such as the whimper of a little puppy.*

Dab and Flick

Kinetic Energy Activity 5: Journal

Let's Draw!

♦ *Draw three kinds of lines that express how you felt during the short, quick, light sounds of the dab and flick.*

♦ *Draw shapes that overlap each other to express how you felt during the sounds of the press and glide.*

♦ *Now, describe the characters you imagined and the moods you felt as you explored these movements. You may use words alone or words and drawings.*

Press, Wring, Glide, Float

Kinetic Energy Activity 6: Gong

To the Teacher

The objective of this activity is for students to feel the movement and hear the sound of the sustained energy of pressing, wringing, floating, and gliding. You will need a gong, cymbal, or other percussion instrument that gives a sustained sound. The symbol for the striking of the gong and its sustained sound will be *—!

Let's Move!

♦ *Find an open space for your kinesphere. Now listen to the gong's one-pitched, sustained, monotone sound *—! It continues to sound for several seconds after I hit it. When I hit the gong the next time, continue moving your arm in one direction using floating, gliding, and stretching for as long as you hear the sustained sound. When you no longer hear the sound, freeze your arm in its position so you control or bind the flow of movement. Some of you will hear the*

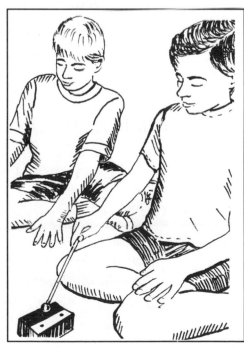

*sound for a slightly longer time because you are closer to the instrument. Ready! Go *—!*

♦ *Now, move a different body part continuously as the gong sounds. This time use firm force and press the air with your body part. Freeze when you no longer hear the sound. Ready! Go *—!*

♦ *Now, try moving only your upper body in one direction for as long as you hear the sound, then freeze *—!*

*Now, choose another body part and move it in a different direction, changing levels *—!*

♦ *What did that feel like? What characters did you feel like? What type of mood did you think of? Did any of you feel like animals? What kind? Plants? What kind? A person? What type of person? [Answers may range from a three-toed sloth to ghosts to kelp in the sea.]*

Sustained Energy

Kinetic Energy Activity 7: Journal

Let's Write and Draw!

♦ *Now relax. Close your eyes and recall any images you had while moving. What were you reminded of? Draw or write about your feelings. You may want to use a combination of words and drawings.*

♦ *Draw at least three kinds of lines to express the feelings you had during the slow, sustained sound of the gong.*

♦ *Draw shapes that overlap one another to express the feelings you had during the slow, sustained sound of the gong.*

Sustained and Quick Energy

Kinetic Energy Activity 8: Kinetic Sculpture

Let's Move!

♦ *Let's have five of you form a group in the center of the room. Decide among yourselves who will be at a high level, who at a low level, and who at a medium level. Now each of you choose how your body will be positioned. Each person should have at least one foot that stays in the same place during the activity. Each person will decide which foot will* *be "glued" to the floor. Let's see some arms and legs in strange positions. Good. Now, when the gong sounds, slowly move one body part for as long as you hear the gong. Keep it moving to the sound. You may have to twist to keep it moving in the same direction. Then freeze. When the gong sounds again, move a different body part. Ready! Go *—! Students, freeze your shape *—!*

◆ *This time let's all divide into groups of five or six. Again decide who will be at high, low, and medium levels and where each foot will be "glued" to the floor. Now, let's all try moving a body part slowly for as long as you hear the sound. Then, when I tap the gong with the stick, like this ***, dab quickly and lightly with one body part. Ready! Go *— ***!*

◆ *Good job. Now, I will alternate using sustained and quick sounds. Make your statues move with the sounds. Ready! Go *— *** —!*

Movement and Sound

Kinetic Energy Activity 9: Sound Screen

To the Teacher

In this activity students will work with partners to create an imaginary Sound Screen between them. One student will simulate touching the imaginary screen while the other will simulate an appropriate response.

Let's Move!

◆ *Today we are going to use movement and voice in an activity called Sound Screen. I will need two people to demonstrate. Face each other and imagine that there is an instrument between you called a Sound Screen. One way to visualize the Sound Screen is as a tall movie screen that makes* 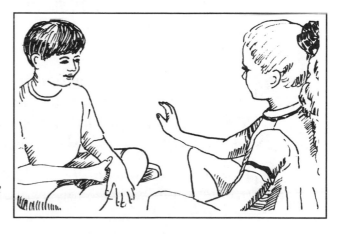 *sounds when touched. One of you will "play" the Sound Screen and one of you will make appropriate corresponding sounds. For instance, if I am making light, repetitive dabbing movements, you would respond with light, repetitive dabbing, sounds. The high part of the screen makes high sounds and the low part of the screen makes low sounds.*

♦ *Two of you come and demonstrate for us. If you play lightly and quickly on the screen, your partner will make light and quick sounds. If you press firmly, your partner will make firm sounds. Give us a few examples. Ready! Go! Good job!*

♦ *Now, we will all try the Sound Screen. Everyone, please find a partner. I will be someone's partner if the number is not equal. Face each other and imagine that you have a Sound Screen between you.*

♦ *A crescendo is a gradual increasing of loudness, intensity, or force. You can create a crescendo by increasing the firmness with which you press the Sound Screen. Now each person "playing" the Sound Screen, make a crescendo by pushing not only with your hand but also with your shoulder or other part of your body. Partners, be ready to make an appropriate sound to the "playing" of the Sound Screen. Ready! Go! Good!*

♦ *Now, show us what it would look and sound like if you were demonstrating lightness on the Sound Screen. Ready! Go! Good job!*

♦ *Now, let's play the TIME continuum. Start with slow, sustained movements and move gradually to quicker, more urgent movements. Begin with a movement that will cause your partner to make a long sound, then move with more sudden movements and sounds.*

♦ *Now, let's work with the SPACE continuum. Move your arm directly from a high position to a low position on the screen. Now, go less directly. Now move your hand in a wavy path across the screen to cause your partner to make wavy sounds of high and low pitches. Keep going less and less directly from high to low.*

♦ *Let's try the FORCE continuum next. Begin with making the lightest, most delicate movements and move toward strong, firm movements. Now, go slowly back to the lightest and most delicate movements. Your partner will choose sounds to match.*

♦ *This time we will explore the FLOW continuum. Begin by making controlled, tight, precise movements. Slowly begin to make more relaxed and freer movements until you are moving extremely freely. Now, slowly move back to tight, tense, controlled movements and sounds.*

The Sound of Art

Kinetic Energy Activity 10: Looking at Art

To the Teacher

The objective of this lesson is for students to begin to see and experience the movement and energy in artwork. Each pair of students will need a reproduction of an artwork. Reproductions of paintings, sculpture, or photographs work equally well. Larger reproductions are better but even post-card size will do. Both *Cu Ra' Tor Express* and *Art Deck*, available from Zephyr Press, have color reproductions that can be used for these activities. One student "plays" the artwork on the Sound Screen while the other student makes a corresponding sound.

Throughout all the activities, it is still important to remember that having a right answer is not the goal. The goal is for students to feel free to respond physically and vocally to what they see. For example, Hartley's **The Aero** (p. 50) has lines that to some students might look and feel like glides, while to others they may look and feel like punches. What looks like a dab to one student may look like a flick to another.

Let's Move!

♦ *Each pair of students will need at least one reproduction of a work of art. Please get your examples and find a space for the two of you.*

♦ *Today we are going to do the Sound Screen in a different way. One partner will "play" an artwork while the other partner responds with an appropriate sound. Let's have one pair of you demonstrate. Bring the artwork you have chosen. Which partner will "play" the artwork and make the movements? Which partner will make the corresponding sounds? Okay, good. Ready! Go!*

♦ *This time when we do the Sound Screen, each of you will play solo. Each person will do both the movements and the sounds for the artwork selected. Let's have a volunteer to demonstrate. Bring your artwork but do not let us see what it is. Place the work before you just like a musician might place music on a music stand. Now, look carefully at your art work and begin making movements that you see in it, as well as the corresponding sounds. This is not easy to do. Ready! Go! Now, show the class your artwork so they can see what guided your movements and voice. Thank you, good demonstration!*

♦ *Now, each person select one or two artworks to play on the Sound Screen. Find your kinesphere and begin.*

Sound Screen

Kinetic Energy Activity 11: Journal

Let's Write and Draw!

♦ *Draw a picture of your Sound Screen and label it with the sounds that you played.*

♦ *Write about how it felt to be a musical instrument that someone could play.*

Voice and Movement

Kinetic Energy Activity 12: Interpreting Drawings

To the Teacher

The objective of this activity is for students to learn to interpret simple drawings through sound and movement. These activities will help students sense the energy in a work of art.

Students will need pencils or markers and paper.

You will need to reproduce and enlarge the five Energy Cards (p. 81-82). Several copies of Energy Card 3 will be needed. Later, you or your students can make your own drawings.

Let's Move!

♦ *Energy can be heard, seen, and felt. Look at card 1. Let's trace the lines and marks in the air and then interpret the card with our voices. We will do this with cards 1, 2, and 3.*

CARD 1

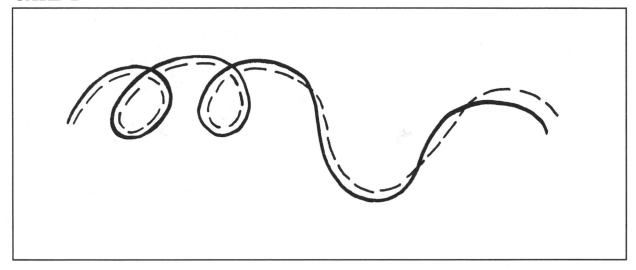

CARD 2

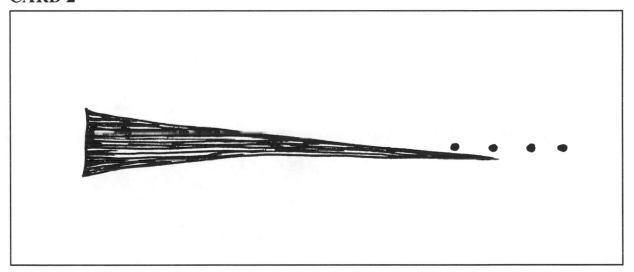

CARD 3

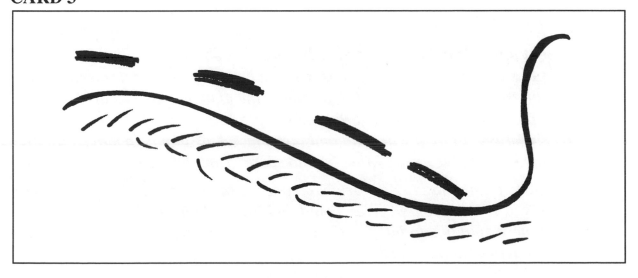

CARD 4

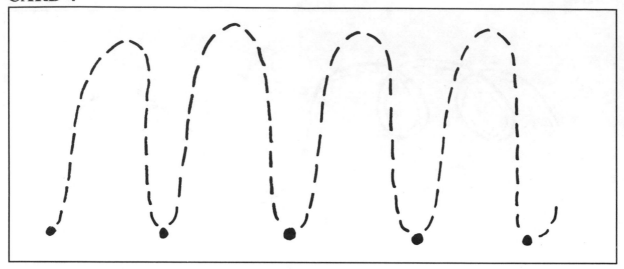

CARD 5

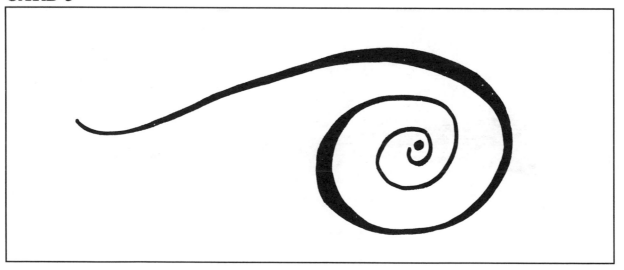

♦ *Now, we will divide into three groups. Each group will "play" a different part of the Energy Card 3. Just as an orchestra has different sections to make different sounds, we will have different sections to make different sounds. Group 1 will "play" the punch lines. Group 2 will "play" the glide and float lines. Group 3 will "play" the dab and flick lines. Each group will read and interpret what sounds to make. Follow my hand as we "read" the "sound score" from left to right.*

♦ *Now, I am going to ask for a volunteer to interpret one of the cards with his or her whole body. You could do it like a dance or like a sculpture. Who would like to interpret one of the cards? Good. Now, someone else interpret another card.*

♦ *I am going to give each of you a blank card on which to draw your own score that you will interpret. After you finish drawing your score, find a partner and interpret your scores for each other with movement only, no sound. Now, switch cards with your partner and interpret your partner's score with both sound and movement.*

♦ *Now, one partner will dance a line of the score while the other partner draws an interpretation of the movement. Make no sounds with this activity. Now change roles, so that each partner has an opportunity to both dance and draw.*

♦ *Next, work in groups of four or five. Each group will need paper [9" x 12" or 12" x 18" will work] and pencils. Each person is to draw a different sound that your group will perform for everyone. We will want to see your score as well as hear it.*

Energy Cards

Kinetic Energy Activity 13: Journal

To the Teacher

In this activity students will draw their own Energy Cards. After the Energy Cards are drawn, students may want to interpret them with music, dance, or voice.

Let's Draw!

♦ *Make a drawing for an Energy Card that you or another person could interpret with a percussion instrument.*

♦ *Make another Energy Card that someone could interpret in dance.*

♦ *Make a third Energy Card that two people could sing together.*

Vocal Interpretation

Kinetic Energy Activity 14: Chicka-Boom

To the Teacher

The objective of this activity is to give students practice in applying the Motion Factors—slow, quick, flexible, direct, light, firm, free, bound—vocally as well as physically. Many summer campers will know the Chicka-Boom chant.

Let's Move!

♦ *We've done several kinds of interpretations. Today we are going to chant in various ways with our voices. Some of you may know the chant. I want you to mirror both my voice and my movements. The first time, I will be slapping my thighs when I say "chicka" and clapping my hands softly when I say "boom." Later we will do different rhythms and different voices and some of you will get a turn to lead. Ready! Go!*

Chicka-boom, chicka-boom.
[Students echo: Chicka-boom, chicka-boom.]

Chicka-boom, chicka-boom.
[Students echo: Chicka-boom, chicka-boom.]

Chicka-rocka, chicka-rocka, chicka-rocka, chicka-boom.
[Students echo: Chicka-rocka, chicka-rocka, chicka-rocka, chicka-boom.]

♦ *Go a little more slowly now. Use your hands in a gliding movement to mirror a ghostlike, monotone voice. Now, let's repeat the chant using that same ghostlike, monotone voice while we continue to move slowly. Ready! Go!*

♦ *Be a little stronger now. Use your arms and fists to mirror the punching strength in your voice. Now, let's do the chant using punching voices and punching movements.*

♦ *Be a little more flexible now. Use your arms and hands to mirror your floating voice, which is changing pitch, up and down, and all around. Now, let's repeat the chant using our floating voices while we move.*

♦ *Go a little more quickly and lightly now. Use your hands near your head and flick and dab them as you chant.*

♦ *Now that you've done the chant many ways, what kind of characters do you think might talk like that?* [Answers may range from mice to ghosts, nervous characters to karate champs.]

♦ *What does a monotone remind you of? See if you get any new ideas while we do the chant in a monotone again.*

♦ *What are some other kinds of voices we could use?* [Answers may range from Donald Duck to Darth Vader.] *Who would like to lead the chant using a different kind of voice?*

♦ *Look at all the reproductions.* [You may use the same reproductions that were used in the previous lessons or choose new ones.] *Select one that has a section that you could interpret with your voice. Don't tell us the one you have chosen. We will try to guess. Who would like to interpret one portion of an art reproduction with his or her voice? Several of you will get the chance to do this.*

Interpretation, Memory, and Mood

Kinetic Energy Activity 15: Journal

To the Teacher

The objective of this activity is to encourage students to transform sounds into graphics. Make reproductions available to students.

Let's Write and Draw!

♦ *Each person will need some drawing paper, a pencil, and a partner. To begin, one person will make vocal sounds while the other person interprets those sounds on paper. Then switch. That way each person will get a chance to both draw and make sounds. You will need to keep the sounds fairly soft so that others can hear their partners. Ready! Go!*

♦ *Select a reproduction and interpret it vocally. Then turn the reproduction around so you cannot see it, and make a sketch of it. The way you draw the artwork is not important. What is important is for you to see how much you are able to remember because of your interaction with the artwork.*

♦ *Now, write about your feelings concerning one of the art reproductions that you interpreted. What kinds of images made the most impression on you? Do they remind you of other things? Are these images connected with the way you feel about the artwork?*

Interpretation and Transformation

Kinetic Energy Activity 16: Be the Thing

To the Teacher

The objective of this activity is for students to have another opportunity to translate from one medium to another. Responding to art in many ways develops understanding, appreciation, and a feeling of kinship with artwork.

You will need to find an art reproduction that has objects or characters that the students can take on as roles. Try to find a copy of Vincent van Gogh's **Bedroom at Arles** or use Ann Rosebrooks's **Kitchen III** (p. 70). You might select several paintings of interiors for this activity. The example we use is Paul Cézanne's **Still Life** (p. 70).

Let's Move!

♦ *Today we are going to do a new kind of interpretation. I will need eight volunteers to become the objects in Paul Cezanne's **Still Life**. Someone will pretend to be the table, someone the pitcher, someone the glass, someone the curtain, someone the platter, and the rest of you the fruit. Come and arrange yourselves so that you look like the shapes of the objects.*

♦ *This first time, each of you will read an example of what the objects might say to one another. Next time, you can improvise the dialogue. Here is the first script.*

Table: I wish he wouldn't use me for these still-life pictures. Look in the drawer. Now he is keeping his paints and brushes there. I used to be a quiet study desk where the worst thing that happened to me was an occasional coffee stain.

Pitcher: Well, I'm just glad to be out of that cabinet. I know I look most becoming with the sun reflecting on my sides.

Fruit: [All read together.] That's great for you but we're going to rot if we sit out here much longer.

Platter: I hate to complain but look at the way he has me tilted. He seems only interested in our shapes, not what we're supposed to be used for. I wish his mother would come in here.

Goblet: I rather like the way he has me picking up a white reflection from you, Platter.

Curtain: And all of you are benefitting from the gorgeous reflection of my beautiful blue self. Shh, quiet, I hear someone coming.

♦ *Good. Now, let's do this same artwork again. May I again have eight volunteers? Select the objects that you will be and arrange yourselves for the scene. This time we will pretend that the occupant of the room has arrived. The objects talk about the person as he moves among them, but he cannot hear them. This time improvise the dialogue.*

Writing Dialogue

Kinetic Energy Activity 17: Journal

Let's Write and Draw!

♦ *Use Rosebrooks's **Kitchen III** (p. 70) or select an art reproduction of an interior of a room. Write a dialogue for the objects found there.*

♦ *Make a sketch of the objects in your own room at home.*

♦ *Write a dialogue of what the objects in your room might say about you.*

Transforming Text

Kinetic Energy Activity 18: Journal

Let's Write and Draw!

♦ *Under the words of the short story below, make lines and marks that would indicate the energy you feel is expressed. You could use one continuous line that moves and jumps or separate lines and shapes. Make your graphic story one that you could interpret in movement, like you did the Energy Cards, because we will be sharing these in class.*

This morning when the alarm went off I quickly jumped out of bed

and dressed. I hurried to breakfast because I could smell waffles

being cooked. I added all my favorite things to my waffle and

began to bite into the crunchy waffle and the sweet syrup.

I totally lost track of time until I heard a car horn honk. I grabbed

my soccer shoes, told my dad thanks for breakfast, and ran out the door.

◆ *This time, make a graphic drawing of the energy of your morning. Can you recall your emotional path this morning as you got ready for school? Were you mentally directed, focused on one thing—such as getting ready so you would be on time? Perhaps the amount of time you had to spend determined how your body and mind were able to move. Did you feel relaxed or urgent about your time? Did you feel free or controlled in your movements? Sketch your morning path from the moment you woke as you bathed, dressed, ate, collected your books, traveled to school, arrived, found your locker or class, and so forth. Your lines may be graphic symbols that remind you of what happened this morning. They do not need to look real.*

Conclusion

Kinetic response to the visual arts is accessible to everyone. Now that you and your students have experienced active art appreciation, we hope you will correspond with us about your experiences. Perhaps we could form a network of kinetic art appreciators!

We hope that you have found a new, vital way to respond to art, as well as sensed the disciplined activity that students must use in order to abstract a sense of energy and movement from visual art. It requires analysis, transformation, synthesis, and interpretation—all of which are demanding cognitive skills. But most important, coming to know works of art through nonverbal communication deepens one's understanding, appreciation, and enjoyment in ways words never could.

Like a kaleidoscope, visual art has many facets and can be interpreted in many ways. We hope you have enjoyed looking at art kinetically.

Glossary

Axis: The imaginary center line from the middle of the head to the point on the ground in the middle of a person's stance.

Bound: Movement flow that can be readily stopped. Also described as controlled, restrained, careful movement effort.

Continuum: An imaginary line along which gradations of time, force, space, and flow can be represented.

Dab: A quick, light, and indirect effort action, as in dabbing medicine on a cut or dabbing paint on a canvas.

Diagonal: Movement from corner to corner in a plane.

Direct: An Effort Element described as single-focused, pinpointed, straight movements in space. Often involves feelings of narrowness.

Directions: Movement can be directed forward, backward, sideways, up and down.

Effort: Mental, physical, or vocal energy that springs from inner impulses, desires, intentions, moods, or drives and results in movement. Every human movement begins with an effort.

Effort Actions: Laban's term for the eight basic movements springing from effort: floating, gliding, dabbing, flicking, slashing, punching, pressing, wringing.

Effort Elements: Laban's term for the sustained, quick, indirect, direct, light, and firm qualities of mind, body, and voice. These are aspects of the motion factors.

Energy: The capacity for action or movement.

Firm: An Effort Element of force (weight) described variously as strong, vigorous, unyielding, and forceful.

Flick: An Effort Action composed of sudden, indirect, light movement, as in flicking off insects, flicking lint off a sleeve, or applying paint with a flicking motion.

Float: An Effort Action composed of sustained, indirect, light movement qualities like the roundabout, buoyant, sustained travels of a balloon or kite.

Flow: A Motion Factor concerned with the degree of liberation produced in movement. Flow qualities range from free to bound.

Force: A Motion Factor with qualities ranging from firm to light movement qualities. Sometimes referred to as weight.

Free: A fluent, ongoing element of motion.

Glide: A sustained, light, and direct Effort Action often associated with the movement of ghosts, skaters, and birds.

Horizontal movement: When we move in the horizontal plane, we move sideways.

Indirect: A quality of movement in space described as wavering, wavy, roundabout, flexible, multifocused.

Inner mimicry: Sensations of emotion and movement in response to artworks. From the German aestheticians of the early twentieth century.

Kinetic energy: Energy associated with motion. "Kinetic" derives from the Greek word "kinein," meaning to move. Kinetic energy can be felt in visual art.

Kinesphere: The space surrounding a person in front, behind, above, low down, and to the sides as far as a person can reach while keeping one foot on a predetermined center spot.

Kinesthetic: Feelings received from the muscles, joints, tendons, organs, skin, and viscera (e.g., the intestines). A source of information about texture, effort, feelings, and spatial position.

Laban: Rudolf Laban (1879-1958), movement analyst, writer, choreographer, and "father" of modern educational dance. *Kinetic Kaleidoscope* adapts and extends his movement vocabulary for use in viewing visual art.

Levels: The low, medium, and high areas in which a body can move in space.

Light: An Effort Element of force described variously as gentle, delicate, buoyant, and yielding. Also described as a fine touch movement quality.

Motion Factors: Laban's term for the four elemental types of motion—time, space, force, and flow.

Planes: Planes are imaginary two-dimensional platformlike shapes that divide spaces.

Press: A sustained, direct, and firm Effort Action, as in pressing a wall or a weight.

Punch: A sudden, direct, and firm Effort Action, as in karate thrusts or jumping on a diving board.

Quick: A quality of time described as sudden and urgent effort and movement. A feeling of momentariness accompanies it.

Safe space (self space, personal space, space bubble): Alternative words for "kinesphere."

Sagittal movement: Forward and backward movements in an imaginary place, called the wheel place.

Shapes: Body positions created, including rounded, twisted, narrow, wide, and angular forms.

Slash: An Effort Action composed of sudden, indirect, and firm movement qualities. Vigorously cutting brush in a jungle involves slashing.

Space: A Motion Factor ranging from direct to indirect use of space.

Sound screen: An imaginary screen or vertical plane separating the space between two people. When one person touches the screen with particular Effort Action, the person on the other side makes a corresponding sound.

Sustained: A quality of time described as leisurely or slow movement. A feeling of endlessness accompanies an extreme degree of sustainment.

Synesthesia: An ability in which one type of sensory stimulation triggers another sense, as in "hearing" color or "feeling" line or "seeing" sound.

Time: One of four Motion Factors Laban used to describe the quality of movement. Time ranges from urgent and quick to sustained and leisurely.

Vertical movement: Upward and downward movement in an imaginary door plane.

Wring: An Effort Action composed of sustained, indirect, firm movement qualities, as in wringing out a towel or twisting and stretching to yawn.

References

Adams, James L. *Conceptual Blockbusting: A Guide to Better Ideas.* San Francisco: W. H. Freeman and Company, 1974.

Arnheim, Rudolf. *Visual Thinking.* Berkeley: University of California Press, 1969.

Boggs, Carol S. "A Consideration of the Weight Factor as an Elemental Feature Common to Both Dance and Painting." Master's thesis, The American University, 1976.

Ghiselin, Brewster. *The Creative Process.* Berkeley: University of California Press, 1952.

Gray, Vera, and Rachel Percival. *Music, Movement and Mime for Children.* New York: Oxford University Press. 1968. The appendix presents movement lessons based on Laban's efforts.

Herman, Gail Neary. *Storytelling: A Triad in the Arts.* Mansfield Center, Conn.: Creative Learning Press, 1986.

Hollingsworth, Patricia, and Stephen Hollingsworth. *Smart Art: Learning to Classify and Critique Art.* Tucson, Ariz.: Zephyr Press, 1989.

Jaffe, Charlotte. *Cu Ra' Tor Express: An Excursion to Appreciating Art.* Tucson, Ariz.: Zephyr Press, 1989.

Laban, Rudolf. *Modern Educational Dance.* 3d ed. London, England: MacDonald & Evans, 1975. Laban presents an analysis of human energy in terms of Motion Factors and Effort Actions. This book strongly influenced *Kinetic Kaleidoscope.*

————. *The Mastery of Movement.* 3d ed. Boston: Plays, Inc., 1971. A book often used by actors to develop movement characterization.

Laban, Rudolf, and F. C. Lawrence. *Effort: Economy in Body Movement.* Boston: Plays, Inc., 1974. This book discusses aspects of effort in industrial movement and in business conversation.

Langfeld, Herbert Sidney. *The Aesthetic Attitude.* Port Washington, N. Y.: Kennikat Press, 1920.

Stanislavski, Constantin. *An Actor Prepares.* New York: Theatre Arts Books, 1936, 1948.

Szekely, George. "Movement as the Basis for Teaching the Arts." *Arts & Activities* (February 1979): 22–25.